MASTERING THE ART OF FREE THROW SHOOTING

Adam Filippi

Filippi, Adam.
Mastering the Art of Free Throw Shooting / by Adam Filippi.

ISBN
978-0-9974261-0-6

This book is available in quantity at special discounts for your group or organization. For further information, contact:

Adam Filippi
www.adamfilippi.com
www.probasketballtraining.com
adamfil@me.com

Printed in U.S.A.
ISBN
978-0-9974261-0-6

Graphic Designer/Art Manager: Lisa Cavallini

All drills, workouts, and exercises contained within this book are for educational use only. It is sold with the understanding that the author and publisher are not engaged in rendering professional services through this book. A competent professional should be consulted should a person wish to pursue professional instruction. The author and publisher disclaim any responsibility for liability, loss, or risk, personal or otherwise, which is incurred as a consequence, directly or indirectly, of the user application of the contents of this book.

Front cover photo by Shutterstock via shutterstock.com.
Back cover photo by Massimo Morri.

Models are Carlton Myers, Adam Filippi, and Cristoforo Cobianchi.

To Jade, the strongest, bravest
and most determined young lady I know.

To Amber, the sweetest girl with the funniest
sense of humor in the world.

To Ally, my little one, whose smile
and laugh lighten up my every day.

… Proud to be your father

CONTENTS

FOREWORD

I am fortunate to have been around the game of basketball for decades as a professional coach and television analyst. The execution of individual fundamentals will always be the foundation for the success of any good basketball team. The skill of shooting was always a priority on my teams and I always hired a shooting specialist as part of my coaching staffs. I don't know how any player or coach can overlook the importance of shooting technique in the game of basketball.

When Adam sent me the draft of his new book, Mastering the Art of Free Throw Shooting, I was intrigued and curious because foul shooting has become such a controversial topic, even at the NBA level. I sat down and read the entire book, "cover to cover", in one single sitting. It was so fascinating and easy to read, transitioning from one subject to another in a natural flow. I congratulate Adam on his thoroughness and simplicity. In teaching, both the visual part and the terminology of instruction that simplify everything in regard to technique, are important. The instructional pictures and the way Adam breaks it down word wise is extremely easy for any individual to assimilate and apply, no matter what age group or level. Adam is a perfectionist who has spent hundreds of hours meticulously analyzing shooting mechanics and developing his teaching concepts and techniques… and only a perfectionist can grasp the little nuances and details of a correct and efficient free throw shot.

Adam, thank you for thinking of me, I appreciate the fact that you gave me the opportunity to read this book! You should feel proud of what you have put together: from the mechanics to the mental side, from the coaching pointers to the drills, you've really hit it all here! This is just an outstanding book!

- Hubie Brown

Basketball Hall of Fame 2005

NBA Coach of the Year 1978, 2004

PREFACE

"How can you write an entire book exclusively on free throw shooting?" If you are asking this question, then most likely you are among the majority of people who consider 70 or 75 percent to be a good free throw percentage, and are overlooking one of the most important elements in the game of basketball. A superficial approach is what allows both players and coaches to accept mediocrity at the free throw line.

The game of basketball has continued to evolve over the past decades, but the only part of the game that has seen no improvements statistically in over 50 years is free throw shooting. I really don't think you can underestimate the importance of free throw shooting in basketball… unless you are satisfied being average or consider 70 percent to be a great statistic! Remember that the term "average" means that you are as close to the worst as you are to the best.

I totally disagree when I hear that the free throw is an easy shot. It may be an easy shot for those who have mastered the art, but in most cases it was not easy for them to reach that level! It's definitely a hard shot for over half the players in the world! Steve Nash and Ray Allen didn't just wake up one day and hit 90 percent at the line; it took them years of self-discipline, dedication, perseverance and perfect practice. Remember "free throws" does not mean you are given "free points": while the shot attempts may be "free" and you have no defender on you, you still need to earn the points! Reaching a level of excellence at the free throw line is a very difficult task to achieve, but the good news is that anyone who understands the mechanics and mental approach involved, and has a plan for development, can do it – ANYONE!

With the release of my previous book, ***SHOOT LIKE THE PROS: The Road to a Successful Shooting Technique***, many questions I received were addressed to free throw shooting and the reasons why it continues to be such a delicate issue for players at all levels. It is no secret to those who know me personally, that the free throw is my favorite shot, as I have always considered it the "mother" of all shots. With so few publications regarding this part of the game, and my constant obsession with free throw shooting, I decided to take the topic one step further and write a book that solely addresses the most unique part of the game of basketball. ***Mastering the Art***

of Free Throw Shooting is the fruit of years of playing, observing, practicing and teaching the game of basketball from youth level to the pro level. During the 12 months it took to write this manuscript, I tried to make at least one hundred consecutive free throws every time I went to the gym. The entire process made writing this book even more challenging, but also very satisfying.

You will find a lot of ***Shoot Like the Pros*** in this book, as the mechanics of shooting and the drills for improvement are obviously the same, but we will go much more in depth in terms of understanding the reasons why you make or miss shots, how to overcome your deficiencies, how to perfect your technique and develop the mindset to become a master free throw shooter. Free throw shooting is by its nature a repetitive act, so I will repeat several fundamental aspects of it throughout the book.

This instructional book is divided in 8 sections: in Chapter 1 you will learn some historic facts on how the free throw has evolved over the years and how it has impacted the game of basketball. Chapter 2 and Chapter 3 explain in depth all the mechanical components of a correct shooting technique and how what we call *shooting rhythm* holds the pieces together. Chapter 4 addresses all the mental aspects and issues of the shot, as developing a positive mental approach will be the key to your consistency. Chapter 5 gives you direction and guidelines to developing a free throw routine that will help guide you through each shot. Coaches will find teaching methods and pointers in Chapter 6. Chapter 7 features shooting drills, exercises, and games to improve at the free throw line. Chapter 8 wraps up the book with free throw pointers, reminders, common misconceptions and other information.

As I continue in my mission of mastering the art of free throw shooting, it is my hope, whether you are a player, coach, teacher, parent or just a curious basketball junkie, that this book can guide you through understanding the progressive steps necessary to become a dead-eye free throw shooter.

Enjoy the book and… Best Swishes!
Adam Filippi

ACKNOWLEDGEMENTS

Writing a book, let alone two, on the skill of shooting, has been no easy task. Putting the words on paper is actually the easiest part! A lot of effort went into this project, including countless hours of observation, research, experimentation, practice, teaching and more.

I would never have been able to complete this book without the help of several people who I want to acknowledge with deep appreciation. First I would like to thank two legendary basketball coaches who have honored me with their endorsements: the great Hubie Brown, a Hall of Fame Coach, two time NBA Coach of the Year (1978, 2004), the game's greatest TV analyst and a world class basketball clinician… what a pleasure just to have had the chance to speak to you; and another Hall of Fame Coach who has supported me in this book from the beginning has been George Raveling, a unique amabassador for the game of basketball whom I have been honored to get to know over the past few years and now understand why he is a mentor to so many. My heartfelt thanks to you both!

Major contributions came from three other people I want to thank. My longtime friend Carlton Myers who graciously posed for the instructional photos throughout the book: you are not only one of the best players and shooters in European basketball history, but along with Kobe Bryant, the greatest competitor I have ever been around. My ever enthusiastic and passionate photographer Massimo Morri, a former point guard and great shooter himself, with whom I go back a long way. My graphic designer Lisa Cavallini, who really brought my words and concepts to life through her vision and talent… I have no idea how I would have finished this project without your artistic eye and patience.

Special thanks to my analytics experts, the Charlotte Hornets' Angus Mitchell and Ben Woldenberg, who provided important statistics and data for the book.

I also want to acknowledge and thank the following people who continue to encourage and support my passion for the art of shooting: Scott Howard, Todd Quinter, Ryan West, Jonnie West, Jerry West, Irving Thomas, Kevin Grevey, Buzz Peterson, Larry Jordan, Matt Doherty, Dickey Simpkins, Masai Ujiri, Pete Philo, Bob MacKinnon, TJ Zanin, Frank Zanin, Ronnie Lester, Lionel Hollins, Jim Shatz, Phil Jackson, Kenny Atkinson, Tommy Sheppard, Mike

D'Antoni, Jim Boeheim, Jim Cleamons, Bill Bertka, Doug Neustadt, Drew Nicholas, Calvin Booth, Giorgio Gandolfi, Fran Fraschilla, Charles Barton, Steve Rosenberry, Lojze Milosavljevic, Ettore Messina, Ivano Zoccadelli, Claudio Crippa, Renato Albonico, Roberto Rocca, Giancarlo Stefanini, Giampiero Ticchi, Roberto Breveglieri, Sandro Gamba, Flavio Tranquillo, Alessandro Mamoli, Simone Pianigiani. Finally, a special thank you to all the players I have had the honor to work with and who I continue to learn from.

INTRODUCTION TO THE SHOT

While shooting is the most important skill in the game of basketball, and its teaching is often overlooked, I believe that despite its importance, the free throw is the most overlooked and under-taught of all shots.

The free throw is the foundation of a correct shooting technique. It is the MOTHER of all shots: both the ultimate mechanical shot and the ultimate mental shot. I have always loved the topic of free throws, and continue believing it is the key shot to master in order to develop correct shooting mechanics, a confident mindset and become a consistent shot maker.

WHAT A FASCINATING PART OF THE GAME!

Basketball is such an exciting game because of its flow, energy, and competitive spirit. Free throw shooting represents a game within the game of basketball, but the real competition is you against yourself, therefore the results are in your own hands. This is what I love about it! It's a big part of the sport, but it is a different shot because its setting occurs in a unique situation. It's a different, special, unusual, but ideal situation to be able to make an uncontested shot with enough time to prepare for it – no defender, no running, no cutting, no catching, no hurry… and no excuses! You can use all of these positive factors to work in your favor or let them work against you. The free throw is perhaps the hardest and most complicated "easy" shot in all of sports. It's such a fascinating part of basketball, where you must combine the technical part with the mental part for a very basic shot.

The setting is ideal, but complicated. The shot is easy, but difficult. The distance is close, but can look far. The goal is wide, but can appear narrow. The ball is light, but can feel heavy. You can have great form, but lack the mental approach. You can have the mindset, but not the technique. You can have both, but can't produce the right rhythm, or do not have a routine to help guide you through each shot. You can't make a free throw without concentration, but too much focus can be just as bad. Why so many headaches for such a basic, uncontested, stand-still shot?

Basketball is a dynamic game played at high speed where your reaction time, instinctive nature and ability to make quick decisions and adjustments prevail. In game situations your shooting motion relies more on reflexes and instincts because you have to catch and shoot as quickly as possible. There is very little thinking involved: you're open, you shoot! The free throw is a less spontaneous shot. At the free throw line you have a large amount of time between the whistle blow and the actual release of the shot. Throw in a timeout perhaps, especially at the end of a game, and by this time your body may have tensed up and your thoughts might have gotten the best of you and the amount of pressure could have doubled in your mind. This type of tension, anxiety and over-thinking is what you want to avoid. Don't let this advantageous setting that gives you the opportunity to capitalize on making 1, 2 or maybe 3 points, work against you: eliminate negative thoughts, stay in the moment, believe in the hours of practice that made your shooting form automatic, focus on the steps of your routine, and sink the shot!

A FAIR SHOT AND A "DEEP" SHOT

What I love about the free throw is that it's a fair shot! It's the one part of the game where there is no discrimination: you can be short or tall, male or female, young or old, talented or limited, a professional player or an amateur, but we are all the same at the free throw line! Nobody has an advantage over another, and the shot's outcome depends only on YOU! It's the only part of the game where you and I can be better than a LeBron James or a Kobe Bryant. I use this concept as a major mental reinforcement with all the players I work with: not everyone can become a star player, but anyone can master the free throw shot. If you can master the basic mechanical part and maintain a certain level of focus, it doesn't matter if you can play the game at a high level or not, you can become an excellent free throw shooter.

In addition to being "fair", there is something "deep" and spiritual related to the shot, something almost religious. I look at the free throw as a "sacred shot". There is a deep emotional and mental meaning to it. Emotional because of all the feelings that may travel through your body when you step to the line: excitement, anxiety, fear, frustration, hope, etc. Mental because if you can master not only the shot itself, but the cerebral state of that moment, dominating all the thoughts and emotions that come with it, your confidence will grow immensely and transfer to the rest of your game. Each player must find the internal harmony that works for him. I just don't see any other part of the game as deep as the free throw.

AN OVERLOOKED PART OF THE GAME

For some reason, when I was a young player, I thought that 80 percent meant being an outstanding free throw shooter. That's what most people continue to believe, and allow themselves or their teams to accept. But, think about it for a moment: missing 20 uncontested, stand-still shots out of each 100 you take is far from great. At the professional level, this means being just slightly above average. Statistical research shows there has not been any significant sign of improvement in free throw shooting in over 50 years at any level. The game continues to evolve, but the game's most basic shot has remained at a mediocre level.

Most of my friends and colleagues continue to tease me because I am so obsessed with free throw shooting and the fundamental skill of shooting in general. To me, it is both a form of self-discipline and, since these days I stay away from playing, also a competitive challenge with myself. If I am not able to shoot for a few days, I feel empty. Exhaustive research, observation and analysis has allowed me to improve both my own shooting percentages and teaching methods at the free throw line. I have reached a pretty elite level of accuracy and confidence, yet I consider myself an amateur compared to some "old school" guys you may have never even heard of, who have set Guinness world records. Facts are that many "senior" shooters are the true artists in this field, which tells me that you never stop learning and improving. You too can become a great free throw shooter!

While I may sound over the top at times, I think you need to be passionate and a bit obsessive to be truly great at something. In basketball you cannot underestimate the importance of proper shooting mechanics and free throw shooting. I have traveled around the world to either watch or teach basketball, and can positively say that very few coaches at any level stress the importance of free throws enough. Most of practice time is dedicated to team offense and defense, preparing for the next big game. Shooting is somewhat addressed, but only superficially on most days and usually in the form of getting repetitions in. Although gym availability and practice time may be limited, I feel that both players and coaches all over the world are taking the easy way out and free throws are simply neglected. Addressing shooting technique can be a sensitive and intimidating subject, but by ignoring one's mechanical flaws and poor free throw percentages you cannot expect improvements. A successful player and/or team must find quality time to address one of the most important aspects of basketball. Free throws make up about 20-25 percent of the total points in an average basketball game. Do you dedicate 20-25 percent of your practice or workout to shooting foul shots? Probably not.

Free throw technique must be a big part of both team and individual practice. Do not cheat yourself or your team! Shooting 10 free throws to end practice is simply insufficient and doesn't produce real results. You must incorporate sets during your practice session to re-create game-like fatigue and stress. If you have any specific mechanical flaws present in your technique, you must find quality time to address and correct them. Repetitive practice of the correct movement enables muscle memory to set in and allow you to develop an automatic free throw motion and routine every time you step to the line.

It is my hope that this book makes both players and coaches recognize the importance of free throw shooting in basketball – not only because better free throw performance leads to improvements in a player's shooting technique, but also because free throws often decide a game's outcome.

BENEFITS OF CONSISTENT FREE THROW PRACTICE

1. **Best Place to Learn Your Mechanics and Practice Them**
   Free throw shooting is the best setting and the proper distance to practice your form, to learn to analyze your own shot, and to make mechanical adjustments. You don't have a defender to disrupt your motion and you have time to prepare for the execution. When you are struggling with your jump shot or in a so-called slump, you should go back and review your basic mechanics and checkpoints. There is no better place to do this than the free throw

line because it allows you to relax, focus, analyze, correct, and regain your normal shooting confidence from an appropriate range and with the right mental approach.

2. **Develops Confidence**

   The free throw line is where shooting confidence develops. Repetitive foul shooting will instill muscle memory and make your shot automatic. You will master a routine where every time you walk up to the free throw line, you will be so confident that you will expect to make every shot. This confidence will transfer to your jump shooting and the rest of your game, as you will be even more aggressive driving to the basket. You will want to draw fouls, knowing that you will score the two foul shots.

3. **Free Throws Win Games**

   When a game is lost by three points or less I always look at the free throws missed. Let's say your team shot 70 percent at the foul line, your opponent shot 85 percent, and you lost by just two points… what do you think? It's amazing how a team can outplay an opponent, but still lose the game because of a superficial approach at the foul line. Analytic studies say that an NBA team may win between 2 and 3.75 more games each season if they improve anywhere from 3 to 5 percent.

4. **A Good Free Throw Shooter Will Get Quality Playing Time**

   Being a good free throw shooter will get you more minutes on the floor and permit you to be on the court at the end of big games. If you are a poor foul shooter, you will probably be on the bench at the end of games; and if you are on the court, your teammates will be reluctant to pass you the ball just in case you do get fouled.

5. **You Can Capitalize At the Free Throw Line**

   You have the opportunity to score more points at the line. The free throw is the one shot where it is allowed to be selfish. Even on a bad shooting night, you can still help your team win by simply hitting your free throws. Also, scoring two free throws early in a game will help you find your groove without having to rush shots. Good one-on-one scorers will drive a lot, draw contact, get fouled, and often find themselves at the free throw line. If they are not high percentage free throw shooters, they become liabilities for their teams. Without selfish intentions, by improving your free throw percentage and becoming more confident, you can easily raise your scoring average 2-3ppg. At the NBA level, during contract negotiations, the money difference between a 15ppg scorer and perhaps an 18ppg scorer can be millions of dollars!!!

WHAT MAKES A GREAT FREE THROW SHOOTER

1. **Knowledge** of the fundamental mechanics and scientific principles involved in free throw shooting.
2. **Application** of all the mechanical components into a fluid motion (shooting rhythm).
3. **Understanding** of the reasons for missed shot attempts.
4. **Capability** of making instant corrections and adjustments. Never miss two shots in the same way.
5. **Simplicity** is the best guide to efficiency. Knowing what is important and what is not. Efficient movements: no wasted time, motion, or energy. Never get caught up in the nonsense (i.e spinning or rubbing the ball, exaggerated number of dribbles, ridiculous routines).
6. **Focus** on the steps that promote the key mechanics of a correct shot, not actually making the shot. Process over product mindset.
7. **Confident Body Language and Approach**: great free throw shooters carry themselves in a confident way like they know they are going to make every shot, and don't get discouraged by a missed attempt.
8. **Routine** as a habit. Same steps every time to enter the comfort zone, and rely on an automatic motion.
9. **Practice Perfection** every day in order to be perfect in games. Great foul shooters have self-discipline and love to practice.
10. **Pride** in accomplishing goals. Aspire to be great, hate to lose, and welcome new challenges.

Your goal is not only to improve your basic shooting technique and reach higher free throw percentages, but also to understand your own shot and become your own best coach. Learning to coach yourself means you have reached an incredibly high level of expertise in shooting that allows you to realize the reasons for missed shots and make instant corrections and adjustments. There is no instant gratification in practicing to improve your free throw shooting. It takes a long time and you should expect plenty of bumps in the road: progress may come only after a brief regression phase, as change often shocks your mind and body. Persistency through self-discipline, dedication, hard work, positive mindset and good practice methods, is what will take you to that next level. Improvement and results always come in a progressive step by step manner.

FREE THROW DEVELOPMENT MODEL

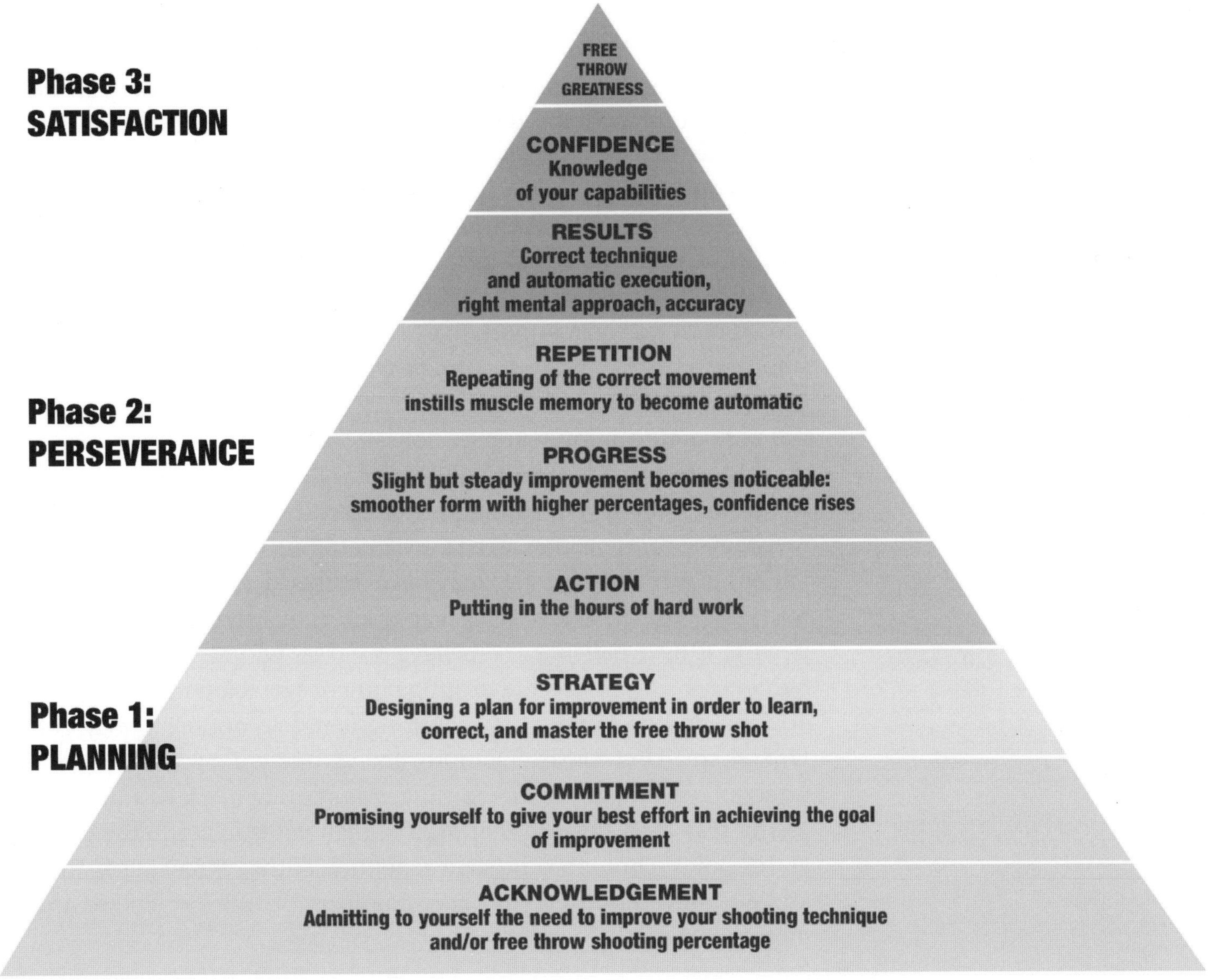
Phase 3:
SATISFACTION
Phase 2:
PERSEVERANCE
Phase 1:
PLANNING
FREE THROW GREATNESS
CONFIDENCE
Knowledge of your capabilities
RESULTS
Correct technique and automatic execution, right mental approach, accuracy
REPETITION
Repeating of the correct movement instills muscle memory to become automatic
PROGRESS
Slight but steady improvement becomes noticeable: smoother form with higher percentages, confidence rises
ACTION
Putting in the hours of hard work
STRATEGY
Designing a plan for improvement in order to learn, correct, and master the free throw shot
COMMITMENT
Promising yourself to give your best effort in achieving the goal of improvement
ACKNOWLEDGEMENT
Admitting to yourself the need to improve your shooting technique and/or free throw shooting percentage

In order to achieve your goal of improving and mastering the free throw shot, you will need some sort of direction. This skill development model is useful to both players and coaches as a reminder that improvement happens over time and in a progressive manner.

1. PLANNING PHASE:
Acknowledgement, Commitment and Strategy

You are either a flawed shooter or are simply looking to raise your percentages. You admit to yourself that you have an incorrect technique or mental approach and commit to working hard (days, months, years...) to improve your free throw shooting. This must be a commitment to yourself, to your coach and to your teammates. Becoming a better foul shooter, you will raise your percentages, expand your scoring game and the team will win more games. You (with the help of a Coach perhaps) design a plan for improvement, a strategy to master the shot and become the best possible free throw shooter you can become.

2. PERSEVERANCE PHASE:
Action, Progress and Repetition

This is both the most important and difficult part of your journey to improve your free throw shooting. After you make the commitment, taking action is not hard: finding a ball and a basket. But in this initial period of training you may not see the improvements or results you expected; you could actually go through a short regression stage, as breaking down your technique and learning and/or correcting the mechanical components can be very frustrating (even more for an advanced player at times). You may have doubts about the plan you are following, lose confidence and may think about giving up. You must persevere, have patience and believe progress will come as you work harder each day. This is the turning point of a development program. You can do two things... and quitting is not an option! Slowly you will see small but consistent improvements and will become optimistic about reaching the goal. Confidence is starting to grow. You begin seeing results in practice that may or may not transfer to the game at this point. Through consistent repetition of the correct mechanics, and a positive mindset, your shooting form becomes smoother and more automatic.

3. SATISFACTION PHASE: Results + Confidence = Success

As you begin to see improvements, and your shot begins to feel second nature, you get more motivated to train every day! Correct technique and repetition through (perfect) practice leads to muscle memory and automatism. Steady improvement leads to measurable results, first in practice and eventually in games. The new skill is now instilled in you, and you are making shots on a consistent basis. Every time you step to the free throw line you carry yourself with a confident attitude, knowing you are a great shooter. Your confidence carries over to your 1on1 game and you are drawing more fouls, eager to score two easy points for your team. You reach your goal of achieving free throw greatness.

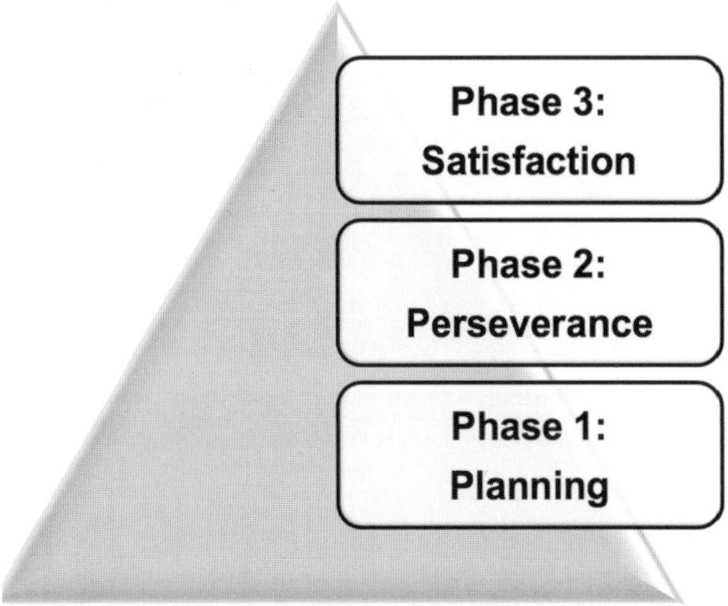

Skill Development Model for Improvement

Chapter 1

GETTING TO KNOW THE FREE THROW: HISTORY AND FACTS

Getting to Know the Free Throw: History and Facts

The great Tex Winter would always begin the first day of training camp asking the new players, rookies and even veterans, some elementary questions about the sport of basketball. While the veteran Laker players would chuckle in the back knowing where the questions would lead, the newcomers would usually be clueless and quiet, just rarely would a new player know a correct answer. Easy questions like "who was Wilt Chamberlain or George Mikan?" would be typical initial questions, but more were the ones about the game's tools and court's dimensions: how big is this basketball? What's its diameter? How much does it weigh? How high is the rim (the only question everyone would always answer correctly)? How far is the free throw line from the rim? How about from the baseline? Initially you would look at it as somewhat comical and absurd, but I soon realized that Coach Winter's intention was to make the players understand the importance of familiarizing themselves with the basic instruments of the game of basketball. So I will try to do the same: giving you a bit of history, listing some fascinating facts that you may not be aware of, and hopefully stimulating your curiosity in order to help you get more familiar with everything that is involved in the free throw shot.

EVOLUTION OF THE FREE THROW

The game of basketball was invented in 1891 by a Physical Education teacher at Springfield College named Dr. James Naismith, who was looking for a way to keep his student-athletes engaged during the winter season. The game was played with a soccer ball and two peach baskets at both sides of the gym. Initially he named the game "Basket Ball" and wrote up the famous "13 rules". Free throws were NOT part of Dr. Naismith's original rulebook.

The free throw was a controversial shot and part of the game from the very beginning and it took over 30 years to determine and establish the rules surrounding it. Naismith's initial idea for a penalty shot was an unguarded 20-foot shot, which if converted, would count the same as a regular field goal. At the time all made

Figure 1.1 *Dr. James Naismith invented the game in 1891.*

baskets were awarded one point. It wasn't until 1895 that we would see the traditional free throw from 15 feet. The following year, Naismith decided it opportune to change the value of regular field goals to two points, and free throws to count one point.

An interesting fact is that for the first 30 years, teams had designated foul shooters, thus the best shooter on each team would be in charge of taking all free throws. In 1924, it was decided that each player who was a victim of an opponent's foul, would have to shoot his own free throws.

Basketball legend Wilt Chamberlain was the reason the free throw rules took another twist. While attending Kansas University, at 7-1 and a tremendously gifted athlete, he was able to dunk his free throws or at least reach very close to the rim. They say that he would basically start from several feet behind the line, then take three giant steps, jump off one foot, and stuff the ball through the hoop or let go of it right before his feet landed back on the floor. So theoretically, it was a perfectly legal shot. In fact, it was Tex Winter, Head Coach at rival Kansas State at the time, who was the main advocate for a rule change. The NCAA decided to modify the rule, establishing that the shooter be required to maintain his feet behind the free throw line throughout the shot delivery, until the ball hit the rim. All leagues around the world eventually adopted the rule.

Over the past few decades the rules involving the free throw have seen additional minor tweaks and changes, for example: technical and flagrant fouls, shooting fouls, "one-and-one" fouls, three shots awarded on 3p attempts, etc. Even today there are slight regulation variations between professional leagues and College basketball, however, the basic rules and violations involved, in addition to the standard dimensions of the rim, the basketball itself, and the distance of the free throw line have remained the same.

EVOLUTION OF THE INSTRUMENTS OF THE GAME

THE BALL

The first ball used in the sport of basketball was a soccer ball. Basketball specific balls were eventually made from pieces of leather stitched together with a rubber bladder inside. In 1942, a molded version of the early basketball was invented. Leather remained the most common material of choice for basketballs, but sporting good brands produce various models of rubber and synthetic composite material balls for all price ranges, ages and court surfaces.

Spalding has led the industry for many years and has been the NBA's official ball since 1983. Since its inception in 1997, the WNBA adopted a Spalding Women's version basketball featuring white and orange leather panels. In 2006, the NBA attempted to change their traditional basketball to a new microfiber composite version, but the result was a total fiasco, as the NBA Players Association fought the change. Players complained that the new ball was too slippery, and that it provided poor grip and also caused cuts on their fingers due to the increased friction. After a sloppy pre-season (we saw a lot of turnovers), the league decided to bring the old ball back.

Other basketball brands, like Rawlings, Wilson, Mikasa, and Molten have also been quite popular over the years in various leagues

Figure 1.2 *The first basketball specific ball, and the 3 modern day professional balls.*

OFFICIAL BASKETBALL CHART

Basketball	Men's Official	Women's Official	Youth Official
Circumference	29.5-30 in. 75-77 cm	28.5-29 in. 72-74 cm	27.25-27.75 in. 69-71 cm
Diameter	9.43-9.51 in. 23.9-24.2 cm	9.07-9.23 in. 23-23.5 cm	8.67-8.83 in. 22-22.5 cm
Weight	20-22 oz. 567-624 g	18-20 oz. 510-567 g	14-16 oz. 397-454 g
Size	7	6	5

around the world and College hoops. The Molten basketball is used in many FIBA leagues, and its design features very particular 12-panel/double-seamed grooves on its surface. Sports apparel companies like Nike, Adidas, and Under Armour are now making highly ranked basketballs (the Nike ball is my personal favorite).

The American Basketball Association (ABA) league, which ran from 1967 through 1976 and showcased the talents of star players like Julius Erving, David Thompson, George McGinnis, George Gervin and many others, used a colorful red, white and blue basketball that you may still see from time to time.

THE BASKET

The first official basket in the sport of basketball was an actual peach basket that was attached to the gym's balcony railing at 10 feet from the floor. Backboards did not exist in the early stages of the game. In the beginning of the 1900s, the fruit basket was finally replaced by the traditional metal rim with braided netting attached to it. The original net was closed at the bottom, so that each time a team scored, players had to interrupt the flow of the game by climbing up to take the ball out. Finally, in 1906, the bottom of the net was cut out so the ball could drop through the goal and teams could inbound the ball more quickly.

A standard basketball rim is 10 feet high (3.05 meters) and its diameter is 18 inches, so just about twice the size of an official men's basketball. Youth/Junior levels may play with 8 or 9 feet baskets, and smaller children may use even lower goals.

For years basketball had a non-flexible iron bolted rim structure that was very hard (would not "absorb" the ball for a lucky bounce) and

Figure 1.3 *The NBA introduced the breakaway rim in 1981.*

became jeopardized by the increased level of athleticism in the game. Breakaway rims were invented in the mid-1970s in order to support the power of slam dunks, avoiding the risk of wrist injuries and a possible shattered backboard. They allow for the rim to bend slightly when a player dunks the ball and then snap back up to its horizontal position. The first version was built with a spring from a John Deere cultivator. The breakaway rim was first used by the NCAA during the 1978 Final Four in St. Louis. The NBA adopted the new rim before the 1981-82 season.

In many parks you find what is called a "double rim", which is a basket structure with one rim stacked on top of another making it very durable and resistant... But so hard, that you must actually swish every shot in order to see the ball go in!

The basket's net that hangs from the rim is usually made out of polyester (NBA, NCAA) or nylon (indoor or outdoor). On many outside courts it is common to find even metal chain nets.

In Naismith's original game, there were no backboards. They were introduced a few years later, not with the intention of facilitating a possible "bank shot", but rather to protect the ball in those gyms where fans could reach it or swat it away from their balcony seats. The first backboards were made out of wood or chicken wire. The regulation backboard is rectangular shaped and measures 72 inches (6 feet) wide by 42 inches high. It is made out of plexiglas so that the audience's view of the game is not obstructed. Non-professional courts and park baskets may have rectangular, oval or fan shaped backboards and are usually made of solid, non-transparent materials. Backboards were initially attached to the gym's walls, but players would not only collide into the wall too easily, but also use it to spring off of to gain more lift off the ground. Backboards were then moved to two and eventually four feet from the baseline and of course 15 feet from the free throw line.

The inner rectangle painted on the backboard's dimension is 24 inches by 18 inches, and although not actually square shaped, it is often referred to as the "square" or "box". The upper edge of the square's bottom line is even with the rim. Although very few players attempt to use the "glass" on their free throws, this square serves as a reference point and may facilitate a "bank shot" from other positions and in other situations.

Figure 1.4 *Regulation backboard.*

THE FREE THROW LANE

The free throw rectangular area is referred to as the lane, paint, or key. It is 19 feet long to the baseline, and 12 feet (3.6 m) wide at the High School/NCAA level, and 16 feet (4.9 m) in the NBA / WNBA / FIBA professional leagues. The free throw line is 15 feet (4.57 meters) from the plane of the front of the backboard: this measurement is often confused as the actual distance from the center or front of the rim. In reality, the foul line is 13 feet from the front rim and 19 feet from the baseline.

The original 1936 lane was called the "key" because of its shape: while the free throw circle was the same, the rest of the paint area was narrower at 6 feet. The NBA's first great center George Mikan, and his effectiveness in the paint, led the league to increase the width of the key to 12 feet, which still stands for High School and NCAA levels. In 1964, during Wilt Chamberlain's dominance, the NBA decided to make a further adjustment, increasing the lane to the modern day 16 feet.

In 2010, FIBA basketball leagues, who had been using a trapezoid shaped lane since 1956, decided to change their shape to the same dimensions as the NBA key.

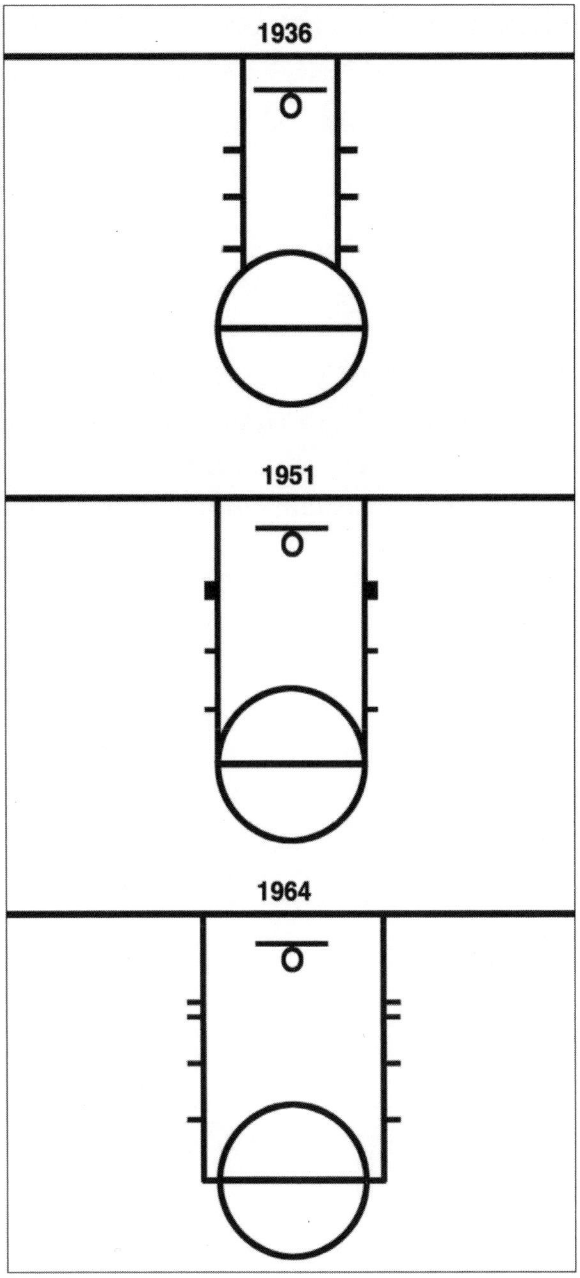

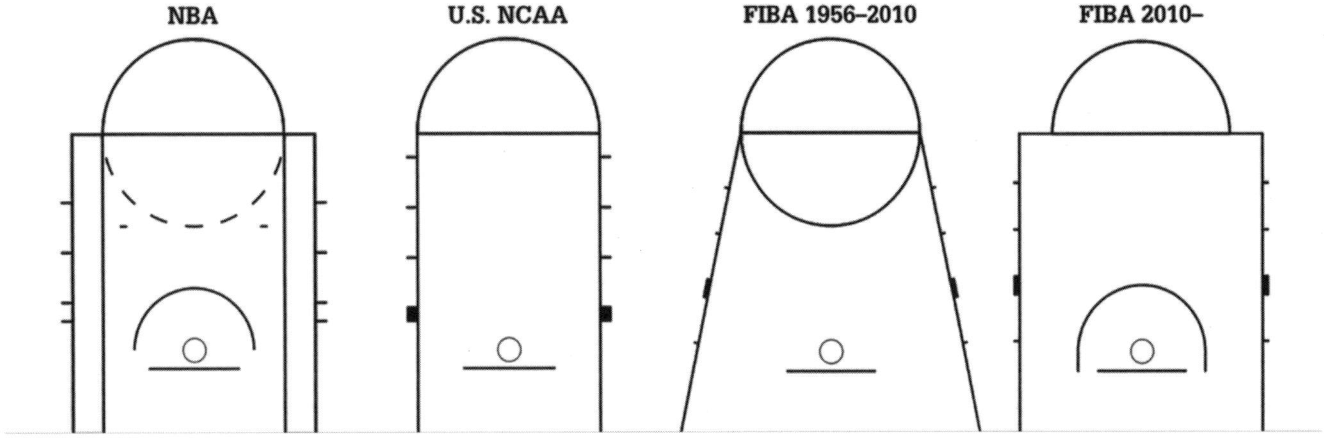

Figure 1.5 Evolution of the free throw lane.

PERCENTAGES BEGIN TO PLATEAU: NO IMPROVEMENT IN OVER 50 YEARS

In the early years of NBA and NCAA basketball, there was constant progress in the game's free throw percentages, but toward the end of the 1950s most leagues and levels of play began to plateau. Statistical research shows that there has been no significant change in percentages over the past 50-plus years, since the early 1960s. The NBA has consistently fluctuated between 73-77 percent, usually maintaining 75 percent as the typical indicator. Men's College percentages have also been consistent, but at a slightly lower 69- 70 percent.

Women's WNBA, whose first season was 1997, actually showed constant improvement throughout its first decade and has slightly better percentages than the men's NBA at this time; data is only based on 17 seasons, but it looks like the WNBA is also finding it's average in the 75-76 percent range. In addition, Women's NCAA has also remained close to the men's average percentages. Like I wrote in my introduction: everyone is the same at the foul line!

Legendary Hall of Fame player and coach, and a mentor of mine during my time working for the Lakers, Bill Sharman (*who passed away as I was writing this book)* became one of the game's best shooters in the 1950s and established himself as basketball's greatest free throw shooter, converting 88.8 percent, which was an amazing feature at the time. It wasn't until later on in the 1970s that the NBA began seeing players reach high levels of free throw shooting again: Rick Barry with his famous underhand technique, Calvin Murphy, Mike Newlin and a few others.

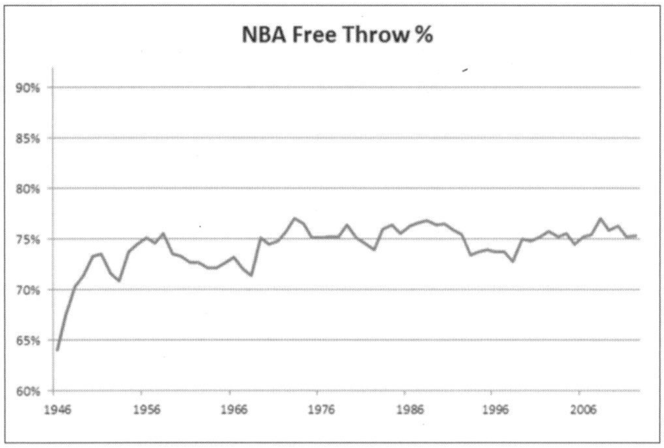

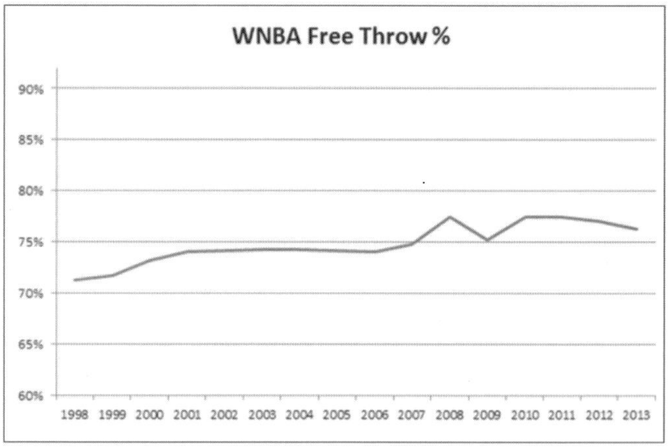

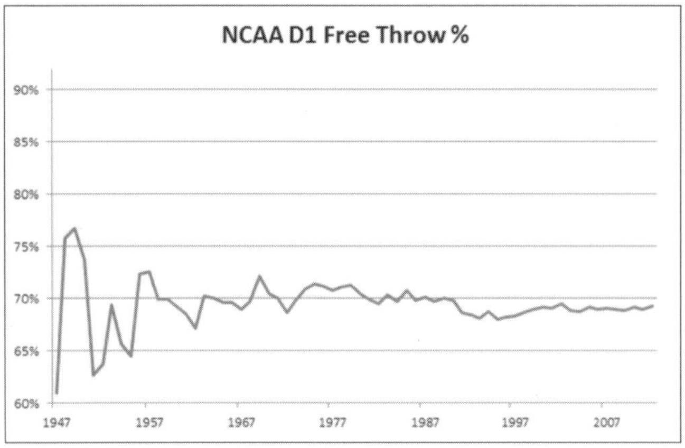

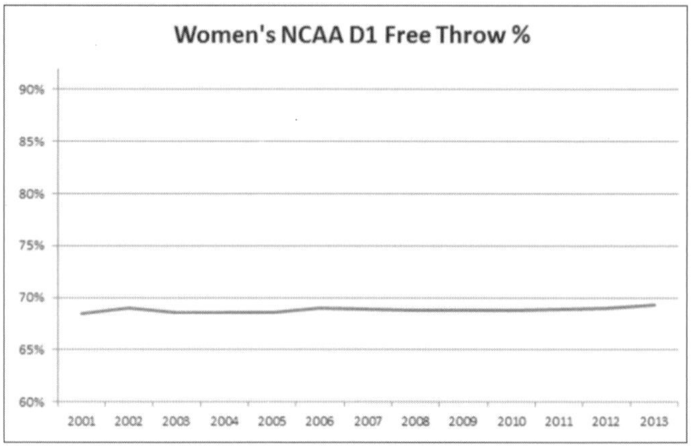

Figure 1.6 *Bill Sharman led the NBA 7 times in free throw percentage.*

In more recent history, star players like Steve Nash and Mark Price set new standards of excellence, with Peja Stojakovic, Chauncey Billups and Ray Allen right behind. During the 2008-09 season, then Toronto Raptor José Manuel Calderon hit an all-time record of 98.1 percent, converting an incredible 151 shots out of 154 attempts from the charity line. If it's true that focus improves with age, when it's all said and done, I believe that Steph Curry will have beaten all records and established himself as the greatest shooter of all time, period.

Although today's professional leagues, from the NBA to the Euroleague, have a higher number of great free throw shooters than in the past, the leagues' overall average percentages have remained approximately the same, as there are also so many poor foul shooters, who in some cases are just an embarrassment to the game not to mention detrimental to their teams. In my opinion, no fundamental basketball skill has a bigger impact on a close game at any level than the free throw. Every week games are lost because of a superficial approach at the free throw line... not necessarily due to mistakes that may occur during the actual game, but because of the lack of attention, commitment and planning given to foul shooting during the week at practice. I feel that anyone can become a good free throw shooter if they are put in a situation to improve and are willing to dedicate the necessary time to achieve successful results.

The fact that the only basketball statistic that has remained consistent over the past 50 years is free throw shooting percentage is a powerful statement, and one of the reasons that led me to writing this book. No improvement in over half a century! Players are stronger, run faster, jump higher, dribble more efficiently, pass with more creativity, shoot from longer distance and with a quicker release. The players, the tools, and the game itself have evolved in countless ways, but the sport's most basic shot has remained at a mediocre percentage. How can this be possible? What does this tell you? Possible reasons include:

- The free throw is one of the most overlooked parts of the game.
- Questionable desire and/or commitment to practice.
- Superficial approach by both players and coaches.
- Not enough practice time or available gym time outside of practice.
- Players and coaches accept mediocrity.
- Coaches tend to address the group more than the individual.
- Players and coaches don't have a plan or strategy for improvement.

NBA ALL-TIME FREE THROW LEADERS AND RECORDS

NBA CAREER LEADERS

Rank	Player	FT%
1.	Steve Nash	.9043
2.	Mark Price	.9039
3.	Stephen Curry	.9000
4.	Rick Barry	.8998
5.	Peja Stojakovic	.8948
6.	Chauncey Billups	.8940
7.	Ray Allen	.8939
8.	Calvin Murphy	.8916
9.	Scott Skiles	.8891
10.	Reggie Miller	.8877
11.	Larry Bird	.8857
12.	Bill Sharman	.8831
13.	Kevin Durant	.8808
14.	Dirk Nowitzki	.8787
15.	Jeff Hornacek	.8770
16.	Earl Boykins	.8758
17.	Ricky Pierce	.8755
18.	Terrell Brandon	.8732
19.	Kiki Vandeweghe	.8717
20.	Darrell Armstrong	.8714

NBA SINGLE SEASON LEADERS

Rank	Player	FT%	Season
1.	Jose Calderon	.9805	2008-09
2.	Calvin Murphy	.9581	1980-81
3.	Mahmoud Abdul-Rauf	.9563	1993-94
4.	Ray Allen	.9518	2008-09
5.	Jeff Hornacek	.9500	1999-00
6.	Mark Price	.9475	1992-93
7.	Mark Price	.9474	1991-92
8.	Rick Barry	.9467	1978-79
9.	Ernie DiGregorio	.9452	1976-77
10.	Brian Roberts	.9398	2013-14
11.	Chris Mullin	.9390	1997-98
12.	Steve Nash	.9378	2009-10
13.	Mahmoud Abdul-Rauf	.9353	1992-93
14.	Ricky Sobers	.9352	1980-81
15.	Rick Barry	.9346	1979-80
16.	Spud Webb	.9339	1994-95
	Stephen Curry	.9339	2010-11
18.	Steve Nash	.9333	2008-09
19.	Reggie Miller	.9328	2004-05
20.	Bill Sharman	.9319	1958-59

Most seasons leading league
7 - Bill Sharman, 1952-53-1956-57, 1958-59, 1960-61

Most consecutive free throws made
97 - Micheal Williams, Minnesota, March 24-November 9, 1993

Most free throws made, none missed, game
23 - Dominique Wilkins, Atlanta vs. Chicago, December 8, 1992

Most free-throw attempts, none made, game
11 - Shaquille O'Neal, L.A. Lakers vs. Seattle, December 8, 2000

Most free throws made, game
28 - Wilt Chamberlain, Philadelphia vs. New York, March 2, 1962 (28/32)
28 - Adrian Dantley, Utah vs. Houston, January 4, 1984 (28/29)

Most free throws attempted, game
39 - Dwight Howard, Orlando vs. Golden State, January 12, 2012 (21/39)
39 - Dwight Howard, L.A. Lakers vs. Orlando, March 12, 2013 (25/39)

Most free throws made, season
840 - Jerry West, L.A. Lakers, 1965-66

Most free-throw attempts, season
1,363 - Wilt Chamberlain, Philadelphia, 1961-62

Most free throws made, career
9,787 - Karl Malone, 1985-86 – 2003-04

Most free-throw attempts, career
13,188 - Karl Malone, 1985-86 – 2003-04

Most free throws made, none missed, game (Team)
39 - Utah at Portland, December 7, 1982

Most free throws made, game (Team)
61 - Phoenix vs. Utah, April 9, 1990 (OT)

Most free-throw attempts, game (Team)
86 - Syracuse vs. Anderson, November 24, 1949 (5 OT)

Highest free-throw percentage, season (Team)
.832 - Boston, 1989-90 (1,791/2,153)

Lowest free-throw percentage, season (Team)
.635 - Philadelphia, 1967-68 (2,121/3,338)

NBA ALL-TIME PLAY OFF FREE THROW LEADERS AND RECORDS

NBA CAREER PLAY OFF LEADERS

Rank	Player	FT%
1.	Mark Price	.9439
2.	Calvin Murphy	.9322
3.	Bill Sharman	.9113
4.	Kiki Vandeweghe	.9073
5.	Hersey Hawkins	.9068
6.	Peja Stojakovic	.9000
	Steve Nash	.9000
8.	J.J. Redick	.8993
9.	Reggie Miller	.8933
10.	Dirk Nowitzki	.8913
11.	Larry Bird	.8903
12.	Brandon Bass	.8902
13.	Vince Boryla	.8889
14.	Jeff Hornacek	.8857
15.	Allan Houston	.8845
16.	Ray Allen	.8835
17.	Wally Szczerbiak	.8824
18.	Chauncey Billups	.8800
19.	Bobby Wanzer	.8797
20.	Jeff Teague	.8765

Most consecutive free throws made
56 - Bill Sharman, 1958-59 Playoffs

Most free throws made in a game
30 - Bob Cousy, Boston vs. Syracuse, March 21, 1953 (4 OT) (30/32)

Most free throws made in a game, none missed
24 - Dirk Nowitzki, Dallas vs. Oklahoma City, May 17, 2011

Most free throws attempted in a game
39 - Shaquille O'Neal, L.A. Lakers vs. Indiana, June 9, 2000 (18/39)

Most free throws made, Career
1,463 - Michael Jordan, 1984-85 – 2002-03

Most free throws attempted, Career
2,317 - Shaquille O'Neal, 1993-94 – 2010-11

Most free throws made in a game (Team)
57 - Boston vs. Syracuse, March 21, 1953 (4 OT)
57 - Phoenix vs. Seattle, June 5, 1993

Most free throws made in a game, none missed (Team)
28 – Phoenix vs. Golden State, May 9, 1989

Most free throws attempted in a game (Team)
70 - St. Louis vs. Minneapolis, March 17, 1956

WNBA ALL-TIME FREE THROW LEADERS AND RECORDS

WNBA CAREER LEADERS		
Rank	**Player**	**FT%**
1.	Elena Delle Donne	.9392
2.	Becky Hammon	.8968
3.	Kara Lawson	.8898
4.	Nicole Powell	.8818
5.	Danielle Robinson	.8782
6.	Kristi Toliver	.8753
7.	Cynthia Cooper	.8713
8.	Seimone Augustus	.8686
9.	Janeth Arcain	.8670
10.	Penny Taylor	.8659
11.	Maya Moore	.8631
12.	Riguna Williams	.8617
13.	Epiphanny Prince	.8603
14.	Sue Bird	.8601
15.	Katie Smith	.8587
16.	Diana Taurasi	.8555
17.	Sandy Brondello	.8541
18.	DeWanna Bonner	.8528
19.	Crystal Robinson	.8500
	Skylar Diggins	.8500

WNBA SINGLE SEASON LEADERS			
Rank	**Player**	**FT%**	**Season**
1.	Becky Hammon	1.0000	2014
2.	Eva Nemcova	.9841	1999
3.	Nicole Powell	.9792	2009
4.	Marie Ferdinand-Harris	.9744	2011
5.	Nicole Powell	.9639	2007
6.	Becky Hammon	.9604	2010
7.	Becky Hammon	.9600	2006
8.	Becky Hammon	.9512	2003
9.	Elena Delle Donne	.9495	2015
10.	Danielle Robinson	.9412	2014
11.	Stephanie White	.9375	2003
	Kara Lawson	.9375	2015
13.	Becky Hammon	.9368	2008
14.	Candice Dupree	.9359	2010
15.	Kara Lawson	.9346	2012
16.	Dawn Staley	.9341	1999
17.	Lauren Jackson	.9340	2008
18.	Nikki Teasley	.9333	2007
	Elena Delle Donne	.9333	2014
20.	Becky Hammon	.9314	2007

Most seasons leading league
6 - Becky Hammon, 2003, 2005, 2006, 2008, 2010, 2014

Most consecutive free throws made
66 - Eva Nemcova, June 14, 1999 – June 5, 2000 (over 2 seasons)

Most free throws made, none missed, game
19 - Elena Delle Donne, Atlanta vs. Chicago, June 24, 2015

Most free-throw attempts, none made, game
8 - Cheryl Ford, Detroit at Charlotte, August 6, 2005 (OT)

Most free throws made, game
22 - Cynthia Cooper, Houston vs. Sacramento, July 3, 1998

Most free throws attempted, game
24 - Cynthia Cooper, Houston vs. Sacramento, July 3, 1998
24 - Tina Charles, Phoenix vs. Connecticut, June 29, 2013

Most free throws made, season
246 - Katie Smith, Minnesota 2001

Most free-throw attempts, season
287 - Angel McCoughtry Atlanta 2011

Most free throws made, career
1773 - Tamika Catchings, Indiana 2002-present

Most free-throw attempts, career
2263 - Tamika Catchings, Indiana 2002-present

Highest free-throw percentage, season (Team)
.855 - Phoenix, 2009

Lowest free-throw percentage, season (Team)
.645 - Washington, 1998

COLLEGE DIV. I ALL-TIME FREE THROW LEADERS

MEN'S COLLEGE DIVISION I CAREER LEADERS					
Rank	**Player**	**FT%**	**From**	**To**	**Last Team**
1.	Blake Ahearn	.9457	2004	2007	Missouri State
2.	Derek Raivio	.9270	2004	2007	Gonzaga
3.	Gary Buchanan	.9127	2000	2003	Villanova
4.	J.J. Redick	.9118	2003	2006	Duke
5.	A.J. Graves	.9005	2005	2008	Butler
6.	Brian Barbour	.8971	2010	2013	Columbia
7.	Jake Sullivan	.8962	2001	2004	Iowa State
8.	Luke Babbitt	.8931	2009	2010	Nevada
9.	Nik Cochran	.8928	2010	2013	Davidson
10.	Donald Sims	.8920	2008	2011	Appalachian State

COLLEGE DIVISION I CAREER LEADERS				
Category	**Player**	**FT%**	**Years**	**Team**
Div. I Men	Blake Ahearn	.9457	2004-07	Missouri State
Div. I Women	Adrienne Squire	.9638	2005-06	Penn State

MOST CONSECUTIVE FREE THROWS MADE – RECORDS BY LEAGUE / LEVEL	
Category	**Player**
Professional	**134** – John Wooden, Indianapolis Kautskys (NBL League), 1930s
NBA	**97** – Micheal Williams, Minnesota Timberwolves, March 24 – November 9, 1993
WNBA	**66** – Eva Nemcova, Cleveland Rockers, June 14, 1999 – June 5, 2000
Euroleague	**94** – Arvydas Macijauskas, Baskonia Vitoria (Spain), 2003-04
College Men D1	**85** – Darnell Archey, Butler University, 2000-2003
College Women D1	**66** – Ginny Doyle, Richmond, 1990-91 – 1991-92
College Men D2-D3-NAIA	**98** – Paul Cluxton, Northern Kentucky, 1996-97
College Women D2-D3-NAIA	**133** – Deb Remmerde, Northwestern College (Iowa) N.A.I.A., 2005-06
High School Boys	**126** – Daryl Moreau, De La Salle (New Orleans, LA), 1/17/1978 – 1/9/1979
High School Girls	**80** – Elena Delle Donne, Ursuline Academy (Wilmington, DE), 2005-06

Now that you have been introduced to the free throw shot and have learned some historic facts, it is time to get to work! Let's take it to the court and address the mechanics for a correct free throw technique!!

Chapter 2

MASTERING PROPER TECHNIQUE: THE MECHANICAL SIDE

Mastering Proper Technique: The Mechanical Side

"You can practice shooting eight hours a day, but if your technique is wrong, then all you become is very good at shooting the wrong way. Get the fundamentals down and the level of everything you do will rise."

– Hall of Fame Player **Michael Jordan**

Whenever I speak at a basketball camp or clinic, I ask the players the same question: who do you consider a good shooter? The usual answers are players like Ray Allen, Steph Curry, Dirk Nowitzki, Kobe Bryant, etc. Then I ask if they all shoot the ball with the same exact form or style. And the answer is obviously NO. So are you trying to tell me that there is more than one way to shoot the ball successfully? Even at the free throw line? Sure. However, most great shooters and free throw specialists share some common fundamental traits, which in most cases can be identified in what I refer to as the "basic mechanical components" of a proper shooting technique. They are:

1. **Balance**
2. **Hand and Finger Placement**
3. **Alignment**
4. **Follow-Through**

In this Chapter we will explain all the intricacies of these mechanical parts, addressing in detail their importance and individual roles in the shot motion. In Chapter 3, you will see how what is called shooting rhythm becomes the binding force that keeps all components together in a fluid motion.

TWO BASIC MECHANICAL PARTS:

1. **Preparation Phase (Loading):** placing feet correctly, flexing knees, cocking the ball, correct hand/arm positioning.
2. **Extension Phase (Pushing):** extension of all body parts – feet, legs, arms, upper body – in a coordinated sequence; wrist and finger flexion finishes the motion.

BALANCE: THE FOUNDATION OF YOUR SHOT

Just as a house's foundation must be strong enough to hold up the rest of the structure, the foundation of shooting a basketball begins with balance. In basketball, without a balanced stance, you will not be able to execute the game's fundamental offensive and defensive skills, and will not be able to react quickly to game situations. The effectiveness of every single skill of the game drastically decreases when you are off balance: from defense to passing, from rebounding to shooting. A good base and compact basketball stance at the free throw line allows you to get "under the ball" with all body parts connected: legs, arms, shoulders, hands, head, and midsection "synched together", in order to gain efficient power for your shot. Maintain balance before, during, and after the shot.

TRADITIONAL STANCE (SQUARED WITH FEET POINTED FORWARD)

At the free throw line you should position your body so it is facing the basket. Your feet should be shoulder width apart with 10 toes pointing at the basket. Although today, many players adopt a slight turn (we will talk about that later in this section) in their stance, most of the greatest free throw shooters in basketball history shot or shoot with their feet pointed straight at the rim. A narrow base with your feet too close to each other will not give you proper balance. A wide foot spread will not allow you to react in game situations, but at the foul line, especially if you are a younger player with limited strength, you may prefer to establish a slightly wider base. Your legs must be flexed at the ankles and knees (don't overbend) because they provide the initial force in the shooting motion. Make sure you are distributing your weight equally on both feet, but never overload on your heels to avoid any negative motion. Don't allow your knees, let alone head and shoulders, to be in front of your toes or you will tend to lean too far forward, and also put your patellar and achilles tendons at risk. Keep a reactive, athletic position even if you aren't going anywhere.

Figure 2.1 *Balanced stance.*

SHOOTING FOOT AND NON-SHOOTING FOOT

At the foul line you have the advantage that you can set your feet without rushing. Some players keep both feet even to the foul line, but I recommend a traditional staggered stance with your shooting foot (right or left, depending if you are right- or left-handed) slightly forward: this is the best way to establish proper body balance, compensating for the fact that you hold the ball on your strong side (right or left) with that shoulder held slightly forward. Position your shooting toe straight, so it is directed toward the goal, establishing a correct shot line. Depending on your body structure and comfort, you may prefer aligning your foot with the middle of the rim, thus placing it in front of the nail that most

Figure 2.2 *Staggered foot stance.*

hardwood floors have in the middle of the free throw line, or just slightly to the side (right if right handed, left if left handed) of the nail (you will read more about alignment principles later in this chapter). Your back (non-shooting) foot's toe should be aligned with the instep of the shooting foot. This staggered foot position, however, may lead you to opening up your stance (after taking a large number of consecutive shots in practice your back foot may tend to open up a bit as your body extends), so your non-shooting foot no longer points forward. It's only natural if this occurs, but you want to keep it under control. You want to be comfortable, but the more the foot opens, the more your hips and, therefore, your shoulders will turn so that you are no longer "facing" the basket. In order to have 10 toes to the rim, your feet should be as parallel as possible. Readjust your feet after each free throw attempt to make sure they are always in the correct position.

BE COMPACT: STAY WITHIN YOUR CYLINDER

Maintaining a compact position is a key aspect in establishing your basketball foundation and your game-like triple-threat stance. Although free throw shooting is a static and no-contact situation, I recommend using the same shooting principles at the line. You must try to reduce movements, eliminating any excess or useless motion of arms, legs, and ball. You want a limited number of body and ball movements, and they must be efficient ones. Don't bend your legs excessively and don't move the ball too much: unnecessary movement leads to increased chance for error. Picture yourself within a cylinder (or I often use the analogy of an old English phone booth): you are confined, but have enough room to operate. Your body parts should be vertically aligned

Figure 2.3 *Compact position with head over base.*

in relation to one another. Don't position your body too low, don't crouch forward too much, don't stand too erect. Your body should be somewhat tilted forward, but still within your base of support. Keep elbows in: close to hips with shooting wrist loaded as soon as you grip the ball. You can "tap" your sides with your elbows just to make sure you are in correct compact position. Keeping your elbows in, close to your body, also helps you establish the correct shot line (which we will address later in this chapter when we talk about alignment) with your shooting arm, and also avoid unwanted pressure from your non-shooting arm.

HEAD AND SHOULDERS OVER YOUR BASE

Being compact and maintaining proper balance is not limited only to your arm, leg and ball movements, but also to your head and shoulders. Your head is quite heavy in relation to the rest of your body and leaning too far out of your base of support (your cylinder) with any forward, backward or sideway head movement, will cause you to lose balance. A good base, with proper foot positioning and strong legs, should allow you to relax your shoulders and not lean back. Keep your head up with your eyes on the goal. Avoid tilting to your sides, as any type of left-right oscillation can cause a misdirected shot. Keep head level with the target and with a slight upward tilt. Maintaining a relaxed neck to avoid any tension, try to keep your head still. Lock your eyes on the rim, do not follow the flight of the ball as looking up will cause you to move your head backward.

SHOOTING POCKET

Staying compact with the ball and not exposing it out of your cylinder is key to your foundation position, but where should you hold the ball? You will find proper balance holding the ball in your shooting pocket region: the stomach-chest area closest to your center of gravity where all movement begins, below shoulders, on your strong side (right or left). This position is key in generating the power to start your shot. Depending on your size, body structure and arm length, your shot pocket height may differ, but I strongly discourage players from beginning their shot motion from too far below their hips, or from the shoulder area as it is very hard to generate enough force and rhythm for a smooth free throw from too high. The combination of correct shooting pocket height (with wrist cocked) and proper use of legs provides the power to initiate the shooting motion. We will get more into detail why the shot pocket is so important in the next chapter as we analyze body coordination to shoot the ball with proper rhythm.

Figure 2.4 *Shooting pocket.*

STRAIGHT STANCE VS TURNED STANCE

Figure 2.5 *Straight foot stance.*

Figure 2.6 *Turned foot stance.*

I believe that your body's natural position is with your feet straight, just like you stand and walk. Therefore, I prefer a traditional basketball stance with parallel feet, 10 toes pointing at the goal, and a squared (always proximal) hip and shoulder position. Most of the best free throw shooters in NBA history shot or shoot the ball with a traditional feet-straight and pointing at the rim stance, just to name a few: Steve Nash, Mark Price, Rick Barry, Ray Allen, Calvin Murphy, Scott Skiles, Reggie Miller, Bill Sharman, Dirk Nowitzki, Jeff Hornacek. However, some players may have trouble finding proper balance, alignment and comfort level and may look to establish a slightly different basketball stance. In today's game we see more and more players adopt a non-traditional turned foot stance at the free throw line. While it is less common than your traditional "feet pointed at the basket" technique, lots of professional players like Kobe Bryant, Kevin Durant, Carmelo Anthony, Dwyane Wade, and WNBA superstar Elena Delle Donne are shooting with their feet not pointed straight at the rim, but turned a few degrees toward the corner of the backboard.

While in jump shooting it is only natural for your body to turn slightly, for free throws it is the initial foot position that matters most, and I believe your feet should be pointed at the rim. Any natural adjustment like a slightly tilted foot position for better comfort is fine as long as it doesn't compromise your alignment. While this is a very subjective topic, I strongly discourage an exaggerated turn in your stance, as in my opinion you are setting yourself up for failure, especially at the free throw line. Unfortunately it is more and more of the "hard turns" that I am seeing, with underwhelming results.

YOUR BODY WILL TELL YOU! *Only a small percentage of basketball players actually need to change their foot stance at the free throw line. I believe that the turned stance should be a natural physical adjustment for those players with particular body structures. Your body will tell you* *if you need to make an adjustment. I do not encourage or teach players to utilize this method unless, because of their personal body structure, it is difficult or uncomfortable for them to get into a traditional stance. The most common case of necessary adjustment is a player with wide shoulders and inflexible upper body (often with a very muscular frame), who struggles to find proper alignment and comfort in the traditional foot stance. In his case, it may be opportune to rotate the feet slightly in order to find better shoulder - eye - arm - hand - ball - rim alignment. However, most young kids who have no need to rotate their stances, are now copying some of the NBA players they see on TV, despite having totally different body types. You cannot predetermine that you want to utilize the turned stance technique simply because Kobe or Melo does. Instead of imitating them, stop and ask yourself why they have modified their basic stance, and most of all, does this apply to you?*

If you are struggling to find proper alignment because of your upper body structure or because you have a balance issue, only then would I try using a turned stance. If not, do not force this position, as you may complicate your shot alignment and motion still further. Adopting an unnecessary turned stance may trigger new flaws or inconsistencies, for example: your elbow rubbing and catching your hip, which will tend to open up (flying elbow), which may then change your hand and finger position on the ball, that eventually may also block your vision of the rim.

In conclusion: your body will tell you if the traditional stance and alignment are not working for you. If you are more comfortable with a slight rotation, so be it. But so far, throughout basketball history, there is no indication that this method guarantees a higher free throw percentage, as it is strictly a comfort issue. Great shooters, turners or not, will make shots regardless.

PERSONAL EXPERIENCE

In my own case, I noticed that my jump shot has a slight natural turn in both my stance and my extension. It is minimal, but as range increases, it is more present. However, at the free throw line I feel more comfortable with my feet positioned straight. I have experimented with both stances, and my percentages remained more or less the same, but the more I turned my feet, the less natural and comfortable my body felt. Based on my personal body structure, a traditional feet-pointed-straight stance works best at the free throw line.

HAND AND FINGER PLACEMENT: CORRECT POSITION AND GRIP ON THE BALL

SHOOTING HAND

Good shooters consistently release the ball straight toward the rim and rarely miss a shot right or left. The goal of the shooting hand is to make the ball go straight as you line up to the basket. In order to do so, you must develop correct, stable hand position to control the ball. Your finger pads should be in contact with the ball, not fingertips nor palm, as you will lose power, feel and control. The ball is not made of glass, so don't be afraid of holding it securely. You have to "feel" the ball comfortably and with confidence: spread your fingers naturally and get a good grip. Don't try to palm the ball because this will cause too much tension – avoid too wide of a "V" between index finger and thumb. Don't keep your fingers too close together because the ball will lay on your palm and you will have no control – avoid too tight of a "V" between index finger and thumb. For a solid, stable grip, you must keep your finger spread consistent, and never move your hand or reposition your fingers on the ball as you raise it. Maintain controlled tension to avoid any type of hand or finger drifting, as it is a sign of insecurity and/or hesitation. You should be able to balance and control the ball with a good shooting hand grip, right above your shooting eye, with approximately 90-degree angles at wrist and elbow. Imagine holding the ball like a waiter holds his tray. I call this your "pedestal" position, where the ball rests on your finger pads and thumb. You don't want any palm in contact with the ball; you should be able to fit two fingers between the ball and palm to make sure there is no contact. When you snap your wrist to release the ball, don't close your

Figure 2.8 *Shooting hand in "pedestal" position.*

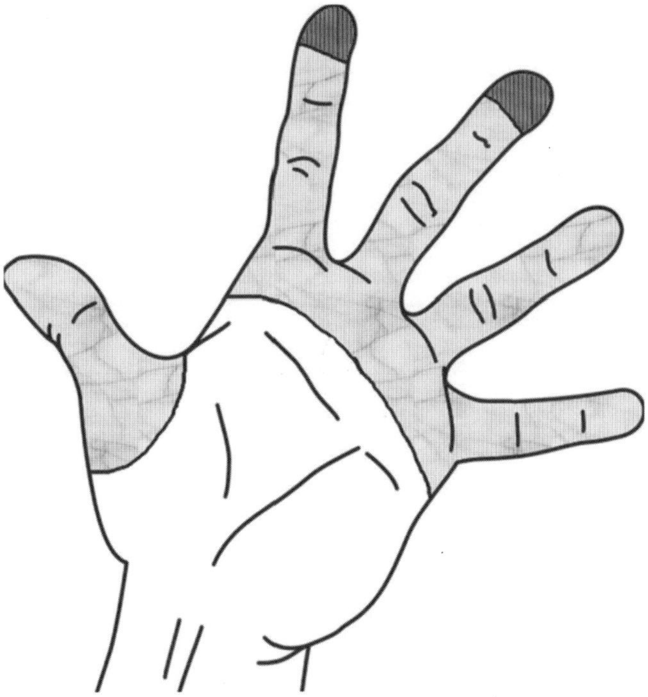

Figure 2.7 *Shooting hand should have no palm in contact with the ball.*

hand because your rotation will be poor and possibly tense. Keep your fingers open – natural spread, no excessive tension – with index and middle fingers in the center of the ball sending it straight toward the goal.

SHOOTING FINGERS: THE "SHOOTING FORK"

The last fingers to touch the ball on its release determine the final force applied, direction, backspin, and "touch" on the shot. Your thumb, index, and middle are the only fingers that have a purpose in shooting the basketball. But which finger or fingers actually release the ball? There has been a lot of talk on this topic and like most of you, I was raised believing that you deliver the ball with your index finger. After I began teaching and obsessively analyzing the art of shooting, I realized that this is a huge misconception. I invite you to both take a look at your own hands and fingers, and to experiment with the ball in your hands. Most players and coaches I talk to say they either shoot with or teach the index finger release; but thinking you shoot the ball a certain way does not actually mean you do. There's a difference between pointing or dominating with your index finger, and releasing the ball with it: although you may point your index finger after the release or as you follow-through, chances are that the ball came off your index and middle fingers. Since your middle finger is visibly longer than your index, I would say it is virtually impossible to shoot the ball exclusively off your index finger. Unless you have very unusual finger length (middle shorter than index) or twist your hand in some unorthodox way, you are releasing the ball off two fingers: your index and middle fingers, which form what I refer to as your "shooting fork". You need to focus on the fork's position in the middle of the ball: at the free throw line you have time to place your two shooting fingers in the middle of the ball with a comfortable spread, forming a tight "V" (about 1" between fingertips; the space in between should be the center of the ball. Practice using the ball's valve stem as point of reference). The "fork" technique not only provides the best control, backspin, and touch on the ball, but it also adds more strength in the wrist flexion during follow-through.

Figure 2.9 *Shooting fork in the middle of the ball.*

OUTSIDE FINGERS: THE "STABILIZERS"

While the thumb, index and middle fingers are your primary shooting fingers, the two remaining "outside" fingers (ring and pinky) of your shooting hand are your "stabilizers". They should be in contact with the ball only for stabilization and must not add any force to the shot. The more active you feel them in the shot delivery, the less accurate you will be. Focus on your shooting fork in the middle of the ball, because any "stabilizer interference" will damage the quality of your release in terms of ball rotation, force, arc, and direction. Remember that the stabilizers' purpose in shooting is only to help you balance the ball in your shooting hand, and they must allow the shooting fork to dominate the ball in order to get a clean release.

SHOOTING WRIST

Whenever you catch or hold the basketball, your hand should always be in ready-to-shoot mode, with your shooting wrist in a loaded position: cocked back at almost a 90-degree angle with your forearm, or enough to see a slight wrinkle in the skin. Proper wrist bend allows you to deliver a correct up and forward shot motion. If your shooting technique does not rely on any wrist loading, chances are you will end up "throwing" the ball either with too flat of an arc, or an excessively high behind-the-head release. Don't keep changing hand, finger and wrist position while holding the ball in your hands as all useless and unneeded movements just increase chances of error and may slow down your release. Do not try to cock the ball back as you raise it up to your release point for your shot because this negative motion might cause the ball to slip backward out of your hands. Develop a firm grip, with wrist loaded and extend your shooting arm straight up and forward toward the basket.

Figure 2.10 *Loaded shooting wrist.*

NON-SHOOTING HAND: THE BALANCE HAND

Most players are able to learn to shoot the ball straight with their shooting hand, but often it is their non-shooting hand that causes interference, disrupting the release. This is a serious mechanical flaw that in most cases generates within a young player who is not strong enough to reach the 10ft goal, but tries to shoot the ball like the professional players he admires. Results are poor shooting techniques, with kids looking for ways to reach the rim using the wrong power sources: throwing the ball from outside their shoulder or behind their head, and most of all, releasing the ball (intentionally or not) with two hands. One of the most common and hardest to correct issues in shooting, this flaw tends to stay with a player even as he grows older. The older a player gets, the harder it is to correct.

Let's analyze the role of this hand in shooting the basketball. You might hear the non-shooting hand referred to as the "help hand", "guide hand", or "off-hand". While I do use this last term, the best description, in my opinion is "balance hand", as its only purpose in shooting is to provide stability while raising the ball during the shot motion. The hand then must gently come off at your release point – ideally the forehead area, above your right or left eye. This hand should not play any part in the release of the ball. Remember, you want a clean one hand shot release. The balance hand should be on the side of the ball, not under and not in front. Balance hand interference is a very common flaw in shooting mechanics: turning

Figure 2.11 *Balance hand on side of the ball.*

Figure 2.12 *Balance hand does not interfere with the shot release.*

your thumb so that it pushes the ball, causing side spin, for example. It doesn't help the shot; it doesn't guide the ball anywhere. Don't let the balance hand put pressure on the ball and make sure it comes off as the shooting arm extends to thrust the ball. You can practice this motion, making the shooting hand and ball slide up and through the off-hand without allowing any friction/dragging. Remember to end the shooting motion with the balance hand and fingers pointing up, opening the gate for the ball as the shooting arm extends. As with the shooting hand, the balance hand has no palm on the ball.

Your non-shooting arm should also be in the right position so as not to interfere with your release. Make sure you remain compact with the off-arm elbow, because if it is popping out too much, it will affect how you place your off-hand on the ball (often with palm), causing unwanted interference, tension or pressure on the release. Don't let the non-shooting arm and hand drop as your shooting arm extends because this movement will cause an imbalance/twist or jerk in your upper body, thus affecting the ball's direction.

COMMON FLAWS CAUSED BY THE BALANCE HAND AND CORRECTIONS

- **"THUMBING"** - Balance hand thumb turns and pushes the ball, causing side spin. This is a very complicated flaw to correct. Keeping your thumb somewhat closed (in contact with side of your index) can help limit unwanted movements.
- **"TWISTING"** - Entire balance hand twists into the shot so your basically shooting a two-handed shot. Try taking your hand off the ball right before you begin to extend your shooting arm.

Figure 2.13 *Thumbing or twisting are common balance hand related flaws.*

- **"DRAGGING"**- Balance-hand fingers drag on the ball. You could be taking the hand off too late, or your fingers are providing too much pressure on the ball. Fingers should be relaxed and placed on the side of the ball. "Open the gate" with fingers pointed up so the ball can exit without being disrupted.
- **"BLOCKING YOUR OWN SHOT"** - Balance hand is in front or on top of the ball, not allowing a clean release. Your hand should always be on the side of the ball, so your shooting arm can extend with no interference.

Figure 2.14 *Balance hand should not be on top or in front of the ball, blocking the release.*

- **"EXTENDING"** - Balance hand is under the ball, almost touching the shooting hand and exerting unwanted force on the ball. Make sure your non-shooting arm does not extend into the shot by pushing the ball.
- **"PALMING"** - Balance-hand palm is in contact with the ball. Avoid tension in hand and arm. Make sure your non-shooting elbow does not pop out as it may cause unwanted palm contact and/or pressure.
- **"DROPPING"** - Balance hand/arm drops as you extend and release the ball with your shooting arm, causing an imbalance, twist, or jerk that will compromise your shot line. Although some players may tend to do this when the ball has already been released, it's still a good habit to keep your shoulders squared to the basket with your non-shooting hand and arm stable throughout your follow-through.

ALIGNMENT: ESTABLISHING YOUR SHOT LINE

All great free throw shooters can do one thing consistently: they shoot the ball straight. In order to establish a stable shot line and eliminate misses to the right and left, you must understand all the components and body parts that lay within the alignment, so you can release the ball straight toward the basket.

IDEAL ALIGNMENT

The concept of alignment is quite simple and obvious, and it is crucial in many sports like golf, baseball, tennis, archery etc. In basketball, it's one of the most important factors in becoming a consistent shooter, especially at the free throw line. Although we strive for perfection, keep in mind that the absolutely perfect shot delivery is an ideal. Perfect alignment is almost physically impossible as our bodies are not designed perfectly. Each player must find his own individual alignment, making his own small adjustments according to his own body structure and comfort. In general, there are some subtle variances among the great shooters, but the farther you stray from strict alignment principles, the less likely you are to become a consistently good shooter.

There are two alignments I address. The first is a very basic vertical line that holds the following shooting components in alignment – right side if right-handed, left side if left-handed:

- **Toe**
- **Knee**
- **Elbow**
- **Wrist**
- **Ball**

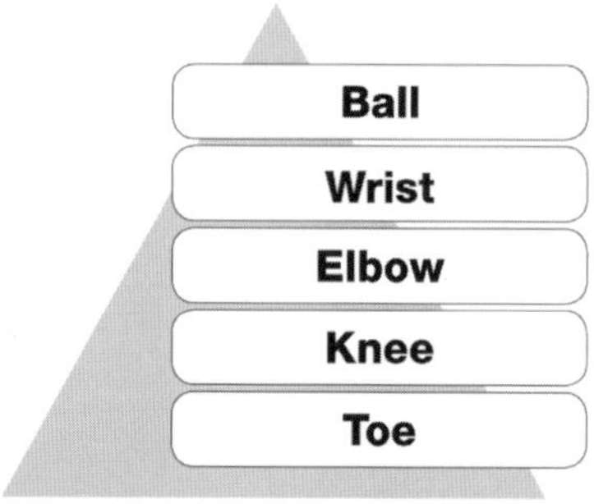

Figure 2.15 *Vertical alignment.*

Figure 2.16 *All components should be in line with the middle of the basket.*

The second alignment gives you a better idea of what we are trying to accomplish in shooting, as it represents your actual shot line, which points the correct direction to the goal. The shot line is determined by a vertical plane that crosses through the dominant side of your body (right for right-handed, left for left-handed) all the way to the middle of the basket. The following shooting components define your shot line:

Figure 2.17 *Proper alignment.*

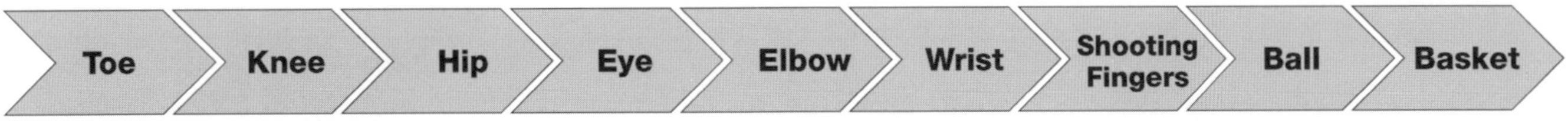

BROKEN ALIGNMENT

In basketball, the mechanical parts of shooting are all closely connected and work together in forms of balance, rhythm (in Chapter 3 we will see how rhythm holds everything together in a fluid motion), and of course, alignment. All it takes is for one component to fall out of place, so that the other alignment parts are consequently affected, and thus cause your shot to be unstable and off target. This is what I call a broken alignment, as it is one of the main reasons why many players have a broken shot. Here are a few common examples of flaws that lead to poorly aligned shooting forms:

- Incorrect foot position triggers a chain reaction of flaws in hips and shoulders, causing discomfort. Shooting toe should lead the way, pointing in direction of the rim.
- Hand and shooting fingers misplaced:
  - Your elbow position and possibly vision are affected.
  - You are forced to make extra movements when you begin raising the ball.

Make sure your shooting fork is placed in the middle of the ball, within the shot line.

Figure 2.18 *Shooting hand and fingers should not be placed on the side of the ball.*

Figure 2.19 *Shooting fork should be placed in the middle of the ball and pointed toward the rim, not to the side.*

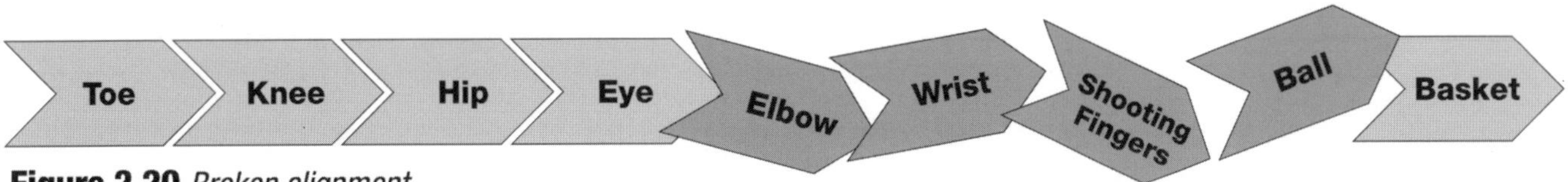

Figure 2.20 *Broken alignment.*

Figure 2.21 *A "flying elbow" can break your alignment and block your vision of the rim.*

Figure 2.22 *Not establishing a dominant side shot pocket will force you to make a crossover motion with the ball.*

- Elbow out (flying elbow) affects the hand and finger positions and possibly vision as you raise the ball. Tap your elbows on your sides to make sure you are compact and shooting elbow is aligned with shooting fork and the rim.
- Weak side shot pocket position causes crossover motion instead of a straight up extension. You will not be able to transfer the force efficiently straight up, and you may also block your vision of the rim. Always get under the ball, gripping it in your shooting pocket area on your dominant side. (note: check if you're a cross dominant shooter – explained later in this section).
- Dropping your shooting arm on your release may lead to destabilizing the last part of your motion. Extend straight up and forward, hold your follow-through.

ELBOW POSITION

Figure 2.23 *Elbow position is key in maintaining alignment.*

Why is the elbow position stressed so much when talking about proper alignment? While sometimes the topic is blown out of proportion, the elbow is one of the most important alignment components; if it falls out of place, it can trigger several other mechanical flaws that will affect your shot line. Here are 4 simple rules to follow:

- Elbow IN, close to hip (no friction) in foundation stance.
- Elbow at a 90-degree angle at all times before the extension.
- Elbow pointed at the rim once you raise the ball to your release point.
- Elbow under the ball at release point (elbow-wrist-ball alignment).

Some great shooters, for example Reggie Miller, have a slight flying elbow, yet they are able to bring it in correctly as their arm extends during the follow-through phase, so they end the shot perfectly in line.

ESTABLISHING THE CORRECT SHOT LINE

Great free throw shooters establish the same alignment every time they step to the foul line. It's part of their routine to get all the components aligned, before shooting the ball: getting your feet placed correctly, gripping the ball in your shot pocket position, extending straight toward the basket, and finishing in a confident manner. In order to do all these things you must know how and where to establish your stance, eliminate any wasted movements, and be able to maintain a consistent shot line throughout the routine.

YOUR REFERENCE POINT

When you catch the ball in action you can afford to be "more or less" aligned, but at the free throw line you have the unique opportunity to establish a perfectly stable alignment with the exact middle of the basket on each shot. Why not take advantage of this? In order to do so, you shoud first establish a correct foot position, using the floor's nail (most wooden floors have a nail in middle of the foul line which is aligned with the middle of the rim) or the middle of the rim as your reference point. Your shooting foot should give the proximal direction, however there are specific details to address in order to find your own personal alignment. Although for years I always aligned my shooting foot with the nail, I readjusted this position once I realized that at my release point (above my shooting eye) the ball was no longer perfectly in line with the middle of the rim. In fact, it is more important that the ball be aligned with the rim as you extend, not your foot.

You just try to shoot every shot the same. As long as my elbow's pointed at the rim, I feel like it has a great chance to go in."

– NBA All - Star **Kyrie Irving**

CHECK YOUR ALIGNMENT BASED ON YOUR RELEASE POINT, NOT YOUR FOOT POSITION OR SHOT POCKET

You can do this test to understand exactly where you should position your lead foot to find your shot line: 1) establish your feet like you typically do; 2) raise the ball to your release point and freeze; 3) check if the ball is aligned exactly above the floor's nail and/or with the middle of the rim (if you have a friend behind you, he can tell you if you are aligned properly); 4) if you realize you are a bit off, adjust your feet so that you do find the perfect alignment from your release point. A perfect shot line helps especially if your shot ends up being a bit short or long and you are hoping for a friendly roll.

Once you realize what works for you, try to find the same alignment every time you are at the free throw line. However, keep in mind that neither all courts nor all rims are the same, so double check your alignment every time you are on a different basketball court.

PERSONAL EXPERIENCE

Each individual player may have a slightly different alignment based on his/her body structure. In my case, my shoulders are not very wide, my eyes are quite close to one another, and my release point is exactly above my right eye. In order for the ball to be perfectly aligned with the middle of the basket when I raise it above my eye, I must move my right foot about 3 inches to the right of the nail so that my shot line is inside my shooting foot. If I did not make this adjustment, the ball would be more aligned with the left side of the rim. It may not seem like a big deal, but any time you have the opportunity to reduce your chances of error, do so.

Figure 2.24 *At your release point, make sure the ball is aligned with the middle of the rim.*

MAINTAIN YOUR SHOT LINE THROUGHOUT YOUR ROUTINE

The concept of shot alignment does not apply only to a "temporary" shooting position, but to the entire duration of the shot motion. In fact, you must maintain your shot line throughout the 3 key shooting positions: foundation/shot pocket position, release point position, and follow-through position.

FOUNDATION POSITION

You must always be ready to shoot in your foundation position. As you hold the ball in your shot pocket, your elbow (near your side), shooting fork, wrist (cocked back), forearm, should always be properly aligned with each other and pointing toward the middle of the rim.

Figure 2.25 *Elbow "in" and shooting fork aligned with the rim in foundation position.*

RELEASE POINT POSITION

As you raise the ball to your release point, in the forehead/eye area, you should have all shot components properly aligned with the middle of the rim: shooting toe, knee, hip, eye, elbow,

Figure 2.26 *Ball should be aligned with the rim once you raise it to your release point.*

wrist, shooting fork, and ball. Once again, since our bodies are not perfect, the alignment is proximal.

FOLLOW-THROUGH POSITION

As you begin the extension sequence, make sure that your body uncoils straight "up and forward" in the direction of the basket. Once the ball is released, make sure you maintain

Figure 2.27 *Hold your follow-through with your shooting fork "inside the rim".*

your follow-through position so that all the shot components remain in line with each other as your shooting fingers finish "inside the rim".

ECONOMY OF MOTION TO STABILIZE YOUR SHOT LINE

Previously in this chapter, we addressed the importance of keeping a compact basketball stance in order to avoid excess movement. Focusing on the strong side of your body, you want to simplify your free throw technique, limiting your movements to reduce chances for errors along the way. Any time you add exaggerated or wasted movements, your shooting mechanics lose efficiency, power, momentum, and your alignment may be jeopardized. Maintain all components in line with each other, do not expose the ball out of your cylinder, and most of all, do not break your alignment with any crossover motion that will complicate ball transfer and vision.

WHEN A TURNED STANCE IS NECESSARY TO FIND YOUR ALIGNMENT

As we addressed earlier in this chapter, there can be potential advantages and disadvantages to a turned stance. While it may help certain players to find an easier shot line, most of the time it just complicates things as one or more components may fall out of alignment. Although your shoulder may align easier with your eye, it may cause some elbow-hip friction, which may then cause you to open up your elbow more, thus changing your hand and finger placement on the ball and resulting in you raising it improperly. Once again, I encourage only players with certain body structures who are uncomfortable with a traditional foot position to make this adjustment in their stance.

EYE DOMINANCE: WHO IS A CROSS-DOMINANT SHOOTER?

Since everyone has a dominant (strong) hand, it follows that they also have a dominant eye. However there are also frequent cases of players who have a cross-dominance, where their master eye does not correspond to their strong hand: so a right handed shooter may have a left-dominant eye and vice versa. Cross-dominance can actually be advantageous in sports where you need to establish a side-on stance, like in baseball and golf. But when it comes to shooting the basketball, things can become quite complex and an ideal shot alignment can be compromised.

The "dominant eye" is the stronger one as it processes and communicates to the brain faster than the other eye. The strong eye is used for aiming, as it judges depth, speed and range, and allows you to focus more accurately than your other eye. A cross-dominant shooter will struggle to find that traditional strong side alignment with all components in line with each other. This can be a tricky matter, and may be what is preventing a player from shooting the ball straight. Here are a few effects that may occur:

- Alignment is broken as your dominant eye is no longer in line with the other key body components.
- Excess movement by your arms, hands, head and the ball because your body is looking to find some way to align itself with the goal.
- Power gets lost loading the ball from one side, crossing your body and face to the dominant eye.
- Vision is jeopardized by the fact that the shooting arm and/or hand may cover one or both eyes.
- Extension sequence may be neither smooth nor straight.

If you realize or have been told you are a cross-dominant shooter, you may have to simplify your shot motion to satisfy both sides of your body. Try to establish a shot pocket, and shot line more toward the middle of your body, in order to reduce excess movements or a body-crossing motion as you raise the ball. Also, you may prefer a quicker and smoother motion, so there is just a limited pause at your release point and your vision is not blocked for an extended time.

ALIGNMENT POINTS AND REMINDERS

- Proper alignment determines your shot line to the middle of the basket.
- The free throw line's nail is your reference point for positioning your feet.
- Keep your feet directed toward the goal.
- Focus on the dominant (shooting) side of your body.
- Your hips should be squared to the basket. If they turn and shoulders remain squared, your elbow might not be able to get through due to friction with your side and might be forced to "fly out".
- Your shoulders should be perpendicular to your shot line.
- Maintain consistent balance and stability throughout the shot motion.
- Keep a compact foundation position: head above waist, elbows near sides, ball in shooting pocket. Keep an economy of motion.
- Elbow in – both of your elbows should always be tucked in near your sides so you are compact and remain aligned. At your release point, your elbow should be under the ball as much as possible. You must be comfortable, so if your body structure doesn't allow this and your elbow is slightly out of line, that's ok, as long as it extends within the alignment as you release the ball.
- Ninety-degree angles – body and arm, forearm and upper arm, wrist and forearm all must be at approximately 90-degree angles.
- Your shooting hand must be positioned correctly, with your "shooting fork" in the middle of the ball and already pointing in the direction of the middle of the rim. If you struggle to place your shooting fingers within the alignment as it causes your elbow and wrist to feel uncomfortable, it's ok to slightly change your index and middle finger position on the ball: slightly to the side, so that when you raise the ball to your release point, with minimal hand and wrist rotation, your shooting fork does fall in line with the other components.
- No "crossover" movements with the ball; maintain consistent strong side alignment.
- At your release point, your shooting hand should be under the ball, not behind the ball.
- It's the position from which the ball is released (release point) that determines your shot line and matters most.
- Shooting consistently straight doesn't always mean that you center the middle of the rim on every attempt, but it does mean rarely hitting the sides of the rim.
- Don't drop either arm as you end the shot motion: extend your shooting arm straight at the rim, maintaining the shot line throughout your follow-through. Don't open up your arms – maintain a consistent window for proper vision.
- Finish with your shooting fork "into" the rim.

Note: remember all ideal angles and alignment rules are proximal, as we are not robots and comfort is most important. However, the farther you stray from basic alignment principles, the less accurate your shot will be.

FOLLOW-THROUGH: FINISHING THE SHOT

"Carrying a project to full completion": this is the English dictionary's definition of the term "follow through", and I feel that it couldn't describe any better what you are trying to accomplish as you finish the shot motion.

To finish your shooting motion successfully, you must have proper follow-through. In many ways this is the most important phase of the skill, as even if you may have an incorrect or unorthodox shooting method, if you break a few of the points we have addressed, a nice finishing sequence may still deliver an accurate shot. This final part of the shot begins as you have gripped the ball correctly, and lifted it up to your release point, above the eye, as your legs begin to straighten. Now you must smoothly extend your arm and snap your wrist. These two final motions will give the last force (both upward and forward), direction, backspin, and arc to the ball.

Let's break down the follow-through components:

EXTENSION – The arm extension, coordinated with the upper body, leg and foot extension, provides the upward force.

WRIST SNAP – The hand and finger flexion provide the forward force. Hand and wrist should be somewhat relaxed yet firm, in controlled tension. You don't want a tense shot, but not a weak shot either. Depending on your feel, you may use either a floppy (loose) wrist snap or a sharper one as long as you are able to forcefully thrust the ball forward in direction of the goal without tension. Relax your body, as your release cannot be too hard or sharp, because should you hit the front rim, it will probably bounce off instead of rolling in softly.

Figure 2.28 *A good follow-through is fundamental in finishing the shot motion.*

DIRECTION – The two shooting fingers, index and middle, should be placed in the center of the ball and should dominate the release, giving the correct direction as the wrist snaps. If you give proper force and have proper arc, your fingers should point down at the end of the snap. I like to say, "put your two shooting fingers into the rim" or "reach inside the rim." However, the final hand and finger position is quite subjective: whether flexed all the way down or level with the floor, what's important is that the ball is released off your shooting fingers and straight toward the middle of the basket.

BACKSPIN – The two shooting fingers are the last parts of the hand in contact with the ball and they provide the backspin that can give that added "touch" on the ball and "roll" on the rim.

> **TOUCH AND FEEL**
>
> The more you practice a correct movement, and the more it becomes automatic, you will also develop more sensitivity in your feel for the ball and the basket. With a good shooter, at some point "feel" and "touch" come into play as he or she may sense something in the shot motion go wrong, and be able to make instant adjustments as the ball leaves the fingers to allow for a good release.

You want a soft rotation so that the rim can "absorb" the ball in case it hits a little iron. While rotation is important, it must be controlled, as excessive backspin leads to a flatter arc: avoid too sharp of a wrist snap, which may cause a strong spinning force on the ball and lead to a hard and flat shot on the rim. At the free throw line, a shot with good rotation, direction and arc will probably go through the basket and the ball will come back to you without you needing to go after it.

ARC – A good and high shooting arc comes from a good follow-through. It's the result of the upward and forward forces, plus backspin. In order to release the ball with proper arc, you must avoid pushing the ball to the rim. Make sure your shooting wrist is loaded, your elbow is under the ball and your shot pocket and release point positions are consistent. Focus on an up and forward motion. You want the ball to go over the front rim and fall more in the center-back rim area of the goal. Studies say the ideal angle of your free throw shot should be in the 50- to 55-degree range, which should allow the ball to drop into the basket from the sky down (the rim would obviously be at its largest if you could drop the ball from right above it at a 90 degree angle). I have always been skeptical when hearing about ideal arc angles, as I believe that it depends too much on distance and player height. Unless you're analyzing video, telling someone to "shoot the ball with a 50-degree angle" does not help, as the last thing players want to hear are numbers that they cannot use in the moment. All you need to know is that a good shooting arc makes the goal bigger: the ball is always the same size and the rim is always at the same height, but the size of the goal does change depending on the entry angle. Remember: the flatter the arc, the smaller the goal.

Keep in mind:

- **Too LOW** of an arc: a flat trajectory usually leads to a hard front or straight back rim miss. Adding a little arc and smoother rotation will soften the shot, and widen the target.
- **Too HIGH** of an arc: there is less ball control, and as it comes down, gravity kicks in, increasing its speed as it drops toward the rim. The result can be a hard miss, instead of the ball dying on the rim and perhaps rolling in. Don't exaggerate your upward extension, but try to balance it with the forward motion.

Elbow Checkpoint – The checkpoint I recommend, that gives the best instant feedback to know if you are using proper arc at the free throw line, is verifying that your shooting elbow extends at least to eye level, or preferably slightly above. If your elbow straightens below eye level the result will probably be a flat shot; if the elbow straightens too far above the eyes you will probably see an exaggerated arc and hard ball on the rim. I like this rule of thumb because it applies to all players regardless of size or age, and by using this method you will understand how to make immediate adjustments on your own. In my opinion,

Figure 2.29 *Elbow should extend above eye level.*

this is both a big teaching point for coaches and learning point for players.

VISION/SHOOTING WINDOW – Correct shooting mechanics should allow you to see the basket properly with both eyes in order to have proper depth perception.

I believe there are 3 visions in free throw shooting:

1. **"Pre-Shot Vision"** – In your foundation stance, after a couple of dribbles perhaps, with the ball gripped properly in your shot pocket region, you will have no problem seeing the basket. This is when you begin to focus on your target and gather the visual information you need to guide the ball to the basket.
2. **"Release Point Vision"** – Once you have lifted the ball up to your eye/forehead area, you should be able to comfortably see the goal underneath the ball, between your arms, with both eyes. This space is your "shooting window", which should remain consistent throughout the follow-through process. Don't allow the ball, your hand, or arm to

Figure 2.30 *Shooting window.*

cover your view of the rim during your shot motion. Not seeing the basket properly may force you to either tilt your head, open your elbow, or move your shooting hand to one side in order to see the goal, and this will compromise your shot line and negatively affect your shot. While an adult player may encounter this problem, a younger player with limited strength may have a release point below the eyes, at chin level, and will continue to have a clear view of the rim. If you are an advanced shooter, because the act of raising and releasing the ball becomes so quick and automatic of a movement, it may not matter if your window is somewhat covered or not: as long as you maintain the basic fundamentals (balance, hand position, alignment, extension) that we have addressed so far throughout the shot motion, you should be able to make shots consistently.

3. **"After-Shot Vision"** – As the ball has been released and you are freezing your follow-through, can you see the goal? Or do you need to move your head to the side or open you arms to get a better view of the ball going in? While the quality of this view may not compromise your results that much, as the ball has already left your hands, I do feel it is important to finish the shot in good balance, holding proper form, and seeing the ball go through the net. This is a major confidence builder.

> **PERSONAL EXPERIENCE**
>
> My technique does not allow the best shooting window. Due to the fact that I have pretty narrow shoulders and a release point exactly above my right eye, my shot line is straight but quite tight. There is a very short instant where my forearm/wrist limits my vision. Nonetheless, I have repeated the motion countless times making it automatic, and maintain correct mechanics so I am still able to shoot the ball efficiently.

Always focus on the rim as you follow through. Don't follow the ball's trajectory as you might move your head; any kind of head jerking (whether forward, back, or side) will affect your follow-through negatively. The only time you will be following the ball's rotation is perhaps when you are learning and analyzing shot mechanics in the beginning stages of development. The free throw is at a distance where it becomes dangerous to raise your eyes to follow the flight of the ball as tilting your head back in order to watch the ball adds negative movement (see next chapter on Rhythm). Although some great shooters do follow the flight of the ball, they usually do it when it is already in mid-air and never when it is just coming off the fingers, and usually on long range shots where there is more air-time.

BODY BALANCE – You must maintain balance throughout the free throw shot motion: before (foundation), during (extension), after (holding follow-through). Neither retract nor fall forward with your head and shoulders during the follow-through. By moving your head too much, the rest of your body will follow. End up in balance on your toes with your upper body just slightly forward as you finish your shot.

FOOT EXTENSION – A good follow-through is not only related to your arm extension and wrist snap. In free throw shooting, the most underrated strength we have is in our feet. By extending your feet you are sure to transfer every amount of positive energy toward the goal in a fluid motion. Maintain your foot extension as you freeze your follow-through, balancing yourself on your toes with your upper body

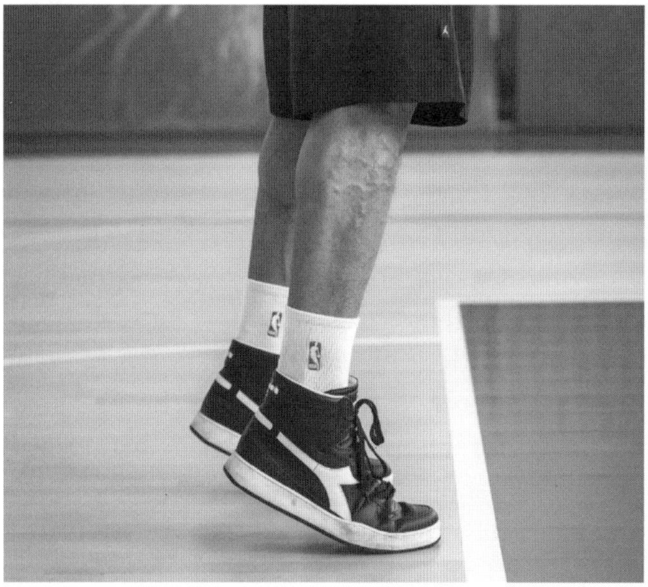

Figure 2.31 *Foot extension.*

slightly forward. This is a key factor in producing positive rhythm and eliminating any negative head or shoulder retraction (*see Chapter 3: Shooting Rhythm*).

THREE REASONS TO HOLD YOUR FOLLOW-THROUGH

Great shooters hold their follow-through. *Freezing* your follow-through is a good habit not only because it enhances a key component of your shooting form in order to make shots, but also because of the following reasons:

1. **Sign of Confidence** – Great shooters carry themselves with a certain confidence. As they release the ball, they are so focused on the act of shooting and the target that they keep their hands up for an extra second or more. Even if a player misses a shot, the fact that he freezes his follow-through is a sign that he is probably still a good shooter.
2. **Can *Fix* Mechanical Errors in a Faulty Shooting Technique** – Anything can go wrong during the shot motion, especially in live action shots when so much comes into play; nonetheless, if you can finish the shot well with an efficient follow-through, you still have a good chance of making the shot. I see countless good shooters with questionable mechanical parts (elbow out, broken alignment, release point behind head, negative motion), who however do finish their shot with great execution, fixing a component that initially was out of place.
3. **Leaves Evidence** – If you drop your shooting arm and hand at your release, it not only affects your release, but it also erases all the evidence in your delivery: if you miss the shot, you can look at your fingers and see that maybe the ball was released off the "stabilizer fingers", or you gave a right/left direction instead of a straight shot at the

Figure 2.32 *Hold your follow-through.*

rim, or perhaps you didn't snap your wrist all the way down. Verifying where the mistake is will make it easier for you (and your coach) to make the right adjustments/corrections going forward.

TARGET AND AIM: WHAT PART OF THE BASKET SHOULD YOU FOCUS ON?

Figure 2.33 *The basket is your target, but what part do you focus on?*

During my basketball life, I have heard too many different and often contradicting instructions regarding where to aim your shot: front rim, back rim, net loops, center of the rim, slightly above the front rim, backboard's square, etc. If a player receives different directions every year from a different coach, he will end up more and more confused. Most of these theories are either non-realistic or totally absurd. Here are the most common aiming point concepts and reasons why I question and do not recommend following them:

- **FRONT RIM:** The player may tend to shoot short, actually hitting the front of the rim.
- **BACK RIM**: How can you aim at a point, that unless the rim is bent down a few inches, you can only see from underneath the goal? While "the idea" of shooting the ball higher and longer toward the back rim is correct, actually "aiming" at the back rim is something different.
- **CENTER OF THE BASKET:** Yes, we do want the ball to go perfectly through the middle of the basket, but the only way to actually aim at the center of the rim would be if you were standing above the 10ft goal and let the ball drop through it. So when I hear "aim at the center of the basket, the bull's eye", I say "how?"
- **JUST ABOVE THE FRONT RIM:** I think we are getting closer to a valid concept, as you want the ball to go above and over the front rim. However, this is still a vague instruction as a player may be too focused on "missing" the front rim, rather than shooting over it.

This is a very subjective topic and there might not be a correct answer: lots of theories and interpretations and so much confusion. The last thing players need is more doubts. In addition, "aiming point" and "focus" are somewhat vague terms in the sport of basketball.

Is an actual "aiming point" realistic in shooting the basketball? Is the aiming point the same as what you focus on? I believe more in something to focus on (image of the ball) rather than a particular point at which to shoot the ball. Since arc and angles are involved and we are not talking about an A to B straight line (like shooting an arrow, throwing darts or even a pass), to me it's unrealistic to aim at a certain point or determine a "bull's eye" in shooting at the rim. I like the idea of *visualization* and *mental* imagery better.

Advanced shooters reach a point where they really don't stop and aim at any particular part of the rim. Their shot is so automatic that the motion has become second nature to them, so they visualize themselves making every shot. But we are talking about seasoned free throw shooters here, not beginners. Young players who are still learning or perfecting their basic shooting mechanics need direction and guidelines in the initial stages of development, and some kind of reference point in terms of aim/target.

So what should you do? I have a different concept which has proved to work as it takes a lot of the doubts and options out of the picture, simplifying the process. I recommend focusing on the goal, but not at a particular part, just the rim as a whole. Try to visualize a clear image of the ball right above the center of the rim, about to drop straight through with a perfect swish: the mental picture of a perfectly straight shot just before the ball goes through the net. Subconsciously, the image of the ball above the rim becomes your aiming point. Every time you locate the rim you should automatically have this positive image in your mind, as it will help you to shoot straight and, most of all, enhance your confidence as visualizing a successful shot is a huge factor in free throw shooting (*we will go more into detail in Chapter 4: The Mental Side*). As you begin to make shots consistently your muscle memory will allow your shot to become so automatic that you will progressively begin seeing the basket twice its size and no longer worry about aiming at any particular part of the basket.

Figure 2.34 *Mental picture of a perfect shot.*

Remember, however, that the concepts of target, aiming, and visualization are among the most subjective matters in shooting, and the bottom line is this: focus wherever you feel most comfortable and on whatever works successfully for you.

SHOOTING DEVICE:
THE "FREE THROW TRAINER"

I was pleased to discover the invention of an extremely useful shooting device, which I fully endorse as it complements my concept in many ways. It's called the "Free Throw Trainer™" (www.freethrowtrainer.com) and helps the shooter to focus by giving indications for direction, distance, and arc.

PLAYERS WITH LIMITED STRENGTH

Standing at the free throw line, the goal is 15 feet away (actually the backboard is) and 10 feet high. This is not an extraordinary distance and height, but basketball rules do not allow you to step over the line. This becomes a problem for young players or ones with limited strength, who rely on momentum and may need to jump slightly forward to reach the rim.

Shooting is the one fundamental skill that can be damaged at a young age if you are not ready to shoot a regulation sized basketball at a regulation 10ft basket. In addition, the free throw line is just too far for some smaller or weaker kids. If you are too small and weak to shoot with the standard tools and dimensions, or perhaps try to compensate by shooting the ball from above your eyes, you may develop an incorrect technique like throwing the ball from outside your shoulder, behind your head or pushing with two hands. Chances are you would be better off on a lower hoop and with a smaller ball. This will allow you to establish correct mechanics that will translate more easily to the standard rim and ball with time. Trying to reach the goal with an incorrect form because of a lack of strength will just complicate your shooting development and the mechanical flaws will carry over to the next level.

A LOWER SHOOTING TECHNIQUE

Not strong enough and need to make adjustments to reach the rim? Great! This is an opportunity to build a more efficient and fluid technique, which will carry over when you are ready to adjust your shot as you grow stronger. Steve Nash, Damian Lillard, Steph Curry and many great WNBA players are perfect examples of outstanding shooters who have maintained scholastic forms as there techniques are quite low, but so fluid and efficient. I feel that players with limited strength often develop a better shot technique because they are forced to adjust their mechanics, searching for the right power sources and getting the most out of them. It is always easier to adjust a correct low shot technique to a higher one as you grow taller and stronger than it is to rebuild your mechanics all over again.

HOW TO COMPENSATE FOR A LACK OF STRENGTH WITHOUT JEOPARDIZING YOUR BASIC MECHANICS:

- **Stay Off the Line** – Position your feet a few inches farther behind the free throw line to make sure you do not step over it as you extend.
- **Wider Base** – Adopt a slightly wider foot stance, a bit more than shoulder width.
- **More Legs** – I rarely recommend excessive

knee flexion at the foul line as it often slows down the shot motion and breaks shooting rhythm. However, it is often useful (especially when you are fatigued) to add just a few degrees to your leg bend.

- **Lower Shooting Pocket** – Your initial position should be lower than the ideal stomach/chest area, so you gain extra power to initiate the shot motion.
- **Lower Release Point** – Begin the extension sequence lower than an ideal "above the eye/forehead" height. One of the main reasons for faulty techniques is players trying to shoot the ball from above their eyes, let alone heads, when they are not strong enough.
- **One-Piece Motion/No Pause** – Your shot motion should be so fluid that the ball goes from pocket position straight through your release point with no pause or hesitation. (*you will see more in Chapter 3: Shooting Rhythm*)
- **Add a Dip** – While coaches insist that lowering the ball is bad, most great shooters actually do dip the ball (especially from long range). At the foul line this action can help you to add extra momentum into the loading sequence. Coordinate the dip with your leg motion and maintain your alignment.
- **Add a Circular Motion** – This is the "super dip". Same procedure as the dip, but you generate even more momentum into the shot, by dipping with a circular "out, in and up" motion. The movements must be coordinated fluidly with your leg motion to gain maximum power, if not it becomes counterproductive.
- **Elbows In** – Both elbows should be near your sides. Keeping your shooting elbow in allows you to establish a correct alignment and transfer all the power straight toward the basket. If your elbow is out, you risk losing some of the strength you have gathered.

Figure 2.35 *Younger kids should adopt a lower shot technique.*

- **Extend Thoroughly** – Exaggerate your follow-through as if you were going up and forward with the ball and into the basket.
- **Foot Extension** – As we addressed during our follow-through: you must not only extend your body, legs and arms, but also get the most out of your feet as they are a very underrated source of power. Push your feet through the floor!
- **Fall Slightly Forward** – Without stepping over the line, extend your body up and forward and follow the trajectory of the ball. With time you will learn to balance and control your body so you do not cross the line.
- **Leave Your Feet if You Must** – This is why you should stand slightly farther away from the line. I am not encouraging you to jump, but if your foot extension forces you to leave the ground a bit, it's OK as long as you do not step on or over the line.

COMMON QUALITIES IN A GOOD FREE THROW TECHNIQUE	COMMON FLAWS IN A POOR FREE THROW TECHNIQUE
• **Balance** – Feet always placed in the same position. Knees flexed, weight distributed on both feet, compact stance.	• Poor balance
• **Fluid One-Hand Technique** – No mechanical flaw in shooting arm/hand.	• Poor grip / hand-finger placement on ball
• **Balance Hand on Side of the Ball** – No interference by balance hand. Fingers straight and pointing up as hand comes off.	• Poor direction from shooting fingers
• **Good Follow-Through** – Finish shot motion with full extension and wrist snap and hold an extra couple of seconds.	• Balance-hand interference
• **Smooth Rhythm** – Body parts extend in an effortless fluid sequence.	• Poor alignment
• **Consistent Shot Line** – Shoot the ball straight. No left or right misses, only miss short or long	• Fading left or right
• **Routine** – Repeat the same ritual every time.	• Lack of power
• **Concentration** – Once locked in, remain focused on the target and don't allow outside distractions. Mechanics should be automatic, not much thinking involved.	• Choppy rhythm
• **Confidence** – Think positively, remain sure of capabilities, visualize every shot going in.	• Poor arc
	• Poor follow-through / instability in extension
	• Negative motion
	• Poor foot extension

"LEARN TO COACH YOURSELF"

If you practice consistently and with a purpose, you will learn how to analyze your own shot proficiently so you recognize the reason for every missed shot. "I felt the ball come off the stabilizer fingers not my two shooting fingers," "I did not extend my elbow," "I didn't get enough push from my legs," etc. A good shooter never misses two shots in exactly the same way, as he can erase the mistake, readjust, and correct for the next free throw. Understanding reasons for misses, learning to read each shot attempt and make instant corrections or adjustments, is a unique ability that separates great free throw shooters from the rest.

MAIN MECHANICAL REASONS FOR MISSED SHOTS AND CORRECTIONS

LEFT or RIGHT MISSED SHOTS	SHORT or LONG MISSED SHOTS
A good shooter learns to eliminate LEFT and RIGHT misses.	**SHORT and LONG misses are often due to a power issue**
SHOOTING HAND is misplaced on the side of the ball and your release causes sidespin. Make sure that you hold the ball correctly, with your finger pads in contact and with the two shooting fingers in the middle of the ball, and that when you reach your release point, your hand is under the ball.	**LEGS** didn't provide enough force. Your lower body must initiate your shot motion. You must flex ankles, knees, and hips to get proper power. Do not overbend your legs, though.
SHOOTING FINGERS flex right or left instead of straight toward the middle of the rim. As you snap your wrist, make sure the ball comes off your index and middle fingers and point in the correct direction.	**POOR GRIP**: You are either providing a weak (short miss) or overly tense grip (you push the ball). Hand should be in "controlled tension".
STABILIZERS (ring and pinky fingers) are the last to touch the ball. Control the ball so that it lies mainly on thumb, index, and middle fingers, with these last two in the middle of the ball, releasing it toward the basket.	**SHOOTING POCKET** is too high. You are not getting enough force from your arms. The lower your pocket, the more power you will achieve. It's OK to dip the ball a bit if you lack proper strength.
FLYING ELBOW: Your elbow is not aligned with the toe, knee, wrist, and ball and not pointing at the rim. You must keep your elbow in at the side of your hip, and as you raise the ball it should be aligned underneath it and with the rim.	**BROKEN RHYTHM**: Your body extends in a choppy manner – a hitch, poor coordination between legs and arms – causing decreased power and fluidity. Begin with your legs flexed and extend them as you raise the ball in a smooth motion.
BALANCE HAND is often the cause for right/left misses. You might be misplacing it either in front of the ball so that it doesn't allow a clean release; or you are twisting your balance hand so that the thumb ends up pushing the ball, not permitting it to go straight. You must keep the non-shooting hand on the side with no tension and end with the hand and fingers pointing up and "opening the gate".	**POOR EXTENSION**: You might get proper force from your legs and possibly even your wrist snap, but you don't extend your shooting arm up and forward. You must extend it up so that your elbow ends above eye level.
POOR BALANCE: Maybe your feet are too close or too wide, or your head is not above your base. Stay low; ankles, knees, hips flexed; feet shoulder-width apart; weight equally distributed on both feet in a compact stance with the ball near your body. Avoid any type of drifting to the side.	**POOR ARC**: Either too low (flat) or too high. Make sure your palm isn't on the ball, that your wrist is cocked back, and that you follow through, giving an up-and-forward force. Don't bring the ball behind your head at release point. Your elbow should end above eye level.
NOT SQUARED UP: Your feet are not positioned correctly and your body is not squared to the rim. This might cause a broken alignment. Keep your shoulders and hips as squared as possible with 10 toes pointed at the rim.	**LATE RELEASE**: Don't shoot at the peak of your extension; avoid any hesitation, pause, or hitch; don't keep too high of a release point; don't bring the ball behind your head. Shoot on your way up as your body extends in a rhythmic motion.
TILTING HEAD LEFT OR RIGHT: You are either off balance or not squared. Poor vision might cause you to move your head to the side in order to see the rim. Your shoulders and feet should be squared to the basket, and your shot window should allow you to see the rim properly.	**NEGATIVE MOTION**: You might retract your shoulders, fade backward, or raise the ball behind your head. These motions will cause your body to move in one direction while the ball is being pushed in the opposite direction (force struggle). You must keep your shoulders relaxed, release the ball above your shooting eye, and extend your body up and forward. Your head, chest, and shoulders should end slightly forward, while you balance yourself on your toes without stepping over the line.

Chapter 3
HOLDING THE MECHANICAL COMPONENTS TOGETHER: SHOOTING RHYTHM

Holding the Mechanical Components Together: Shooting Rhythm

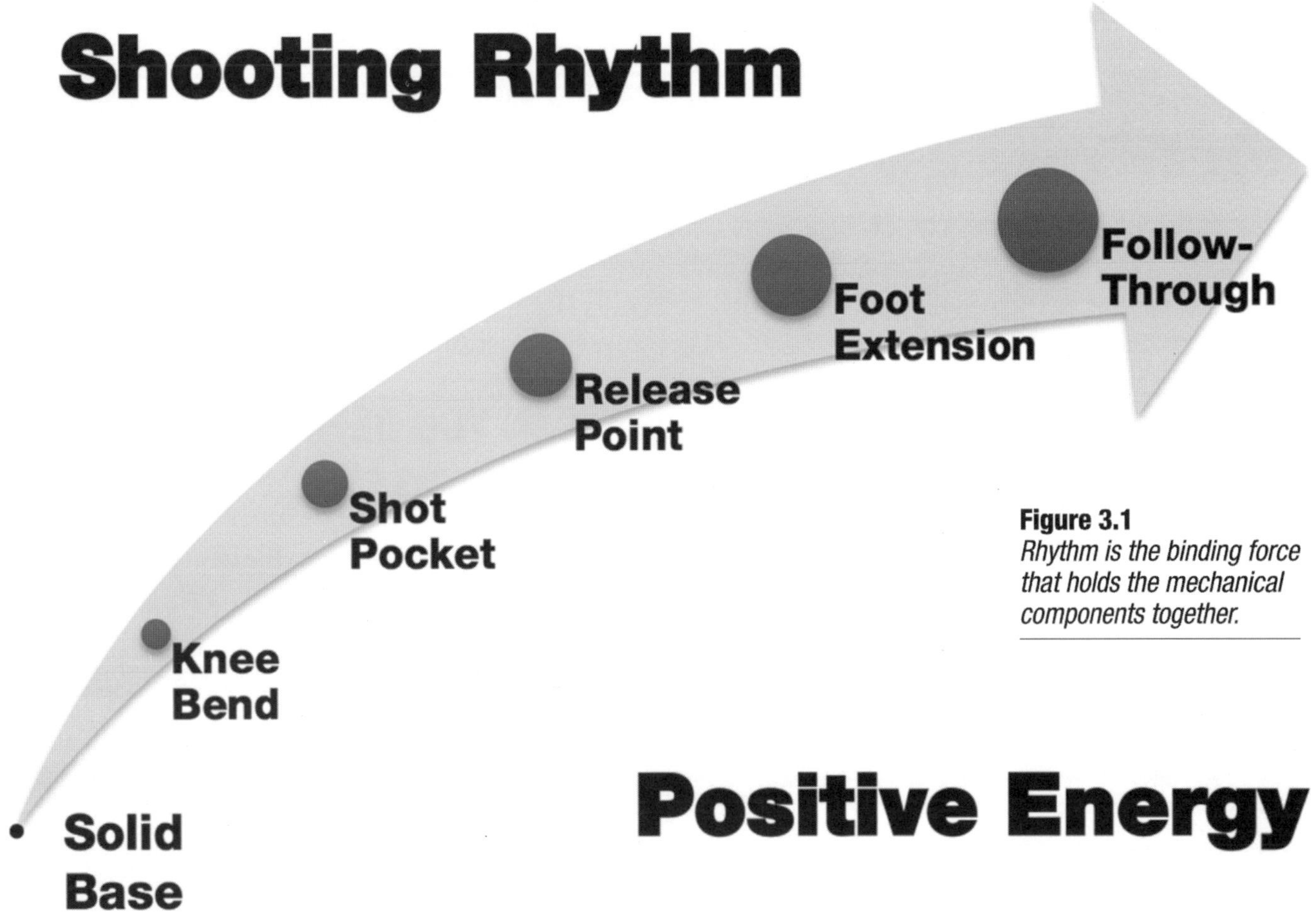

Figure 3.1
Rhythm is the binding force that holds the mechanical components together.

The free throw is a "rhythmic shot". Not that the other game shots don't require rhythm, but it's often the game's speed, dribbling and cutting actions that allow your movements' inertia and momentum to help create the necessary rhythm for a fluid and coordinated shot. With a stationary shot like the free throw, where there is no momentum and your feet don't leave the ground, it is a bit different: you must generate a fluid motion from a static/stationary body position, which is not easy for most players, and in some cases may be more difficult than with a typical game shot.

Rhythm is a vague term. What makes sense to one person may not make sense to another. Not all players interpret the concept of rhythm

Figure 3.2 *The coordination between the leg and arm motions generates positive rhythm.*

in the same way as you may, and the same can be said for coaches. Because a coach cannot feel what another person is feeling, I find the concept of rhythm very difficult to explain, teach and learn with players at any level. You cannot expect each player to adapt as easily as others, because personal coordination and physical characteristics play a big role in the shooting motion. Therefore, rhythm becomes a very subjective matter and it should develop within each individual player. Some coaches do not put much emphasis on the concept of rhythm, saying that having rhythm just means your mechanics are efficient. I think there is more to it than just that. In this chapter we will try to explain better what rhythm is, and how important it is in free throw shooting.

CAN YOU DEFINE RHYTHM?

I once heard a coach define shooting rhythm as "something hard to explain in words as it generates deep in the body". While I understand his thoughts, I will offer you my reflections, concepts and definition in words, in hopes of giving you a more concrete idea of a

Average NBA Free Throw Percentages by Player Height

Height Range	Free Throw %
< 6 feet	81.7 %
6'0" – 6'4"	79.9 %
6'5" – 6'8"	76.9 %
6'9" – 7'0"	71.3 %
> 7 feet	67.8 %

NBA data since 1990

very complicated topic.

I would describe body rhythm as the coordination between the leg motion and arm motion, stabilized by the body's core musculature. In the previous chapter we discussed and analyzed the roles of the feet, knees, elbows, arms, hands, and fingers during the shot motion. The binding force that holds all components together in a fluid motion is rhythm. Your shooting rhythm is a combination of your natural body motion with the components and ball positions of a correct shot technique. Smooth rhythm is what allows a seemingly fragile 6-2 guard like Steph Curry to shoot from deep range with no strain or effort. On the contrary, a tense or choppy rhythm is what keeps big strong and muscular players like Shaquille O'Neil, Ben Wallace and Dwight Howard from being able to deliver a consistent, soft and accurate free throw shot. In general, taller players are often more challenged at finding their coordination to develop rhythm in their shooting stroke.

Your legs, arms, shoulders, hands, head and mid-section must be connected (I like to say in synch) in order to produce smooth mechanics. Rhythm is created through the coordination between your leg motion and arm motion, allowing a fluid and comfortable shooting technique. Efficient leg and arm motions generate the needed power for your shot, so you don't have to search for additional strength with compensations, which may compromise the quality of your mechanics. Your movements should be power-producing and excess-motion-saving.

Your legs begin the shot motion, providing the initial push. You must not raise the ball as you flex your knees, but keep it in your shooting pocket. When players raise the ball as they flex their knees, this can chop rhythm and momentum and slow down the motion. Remember that the coordination between your legs and arms is the key to a smooth motion. You want to begin your free throw motion already with a slight knee bend, and have every element go up together. All angles open up in a fluid sequence. Shooting wrist and finger flexion (follow-through) end the rhythmic motion. Head and shoulders must be relaxed so they can "get into" the release. At the end of the shot, your body should be inclined very slightly forward, never falling back (negative motion).

SHOOTING RHYTHM		
Leg Motion	*Coordination*	**Arm Motion**
Solid Base		Shooting Pocket
Knee Bend	stabilized by the body's **CORE**	Release Point
Foot Extension		Follow-Through
Lower Body	*Mid-Section*	*Upper Body*

LEG MOTION

In order to produce positive rhythm, your lower body motion must begin with a solid, balanced foundation and a certain degree of knee flexion. Even during a static shot like the free throw, your legs should always be in a reactive/athletic position ready to extend. Standing flat footed (weight on your heels), with your legs completely straight takes all momentum and positive energy out of your body movements. I don't recommend excessive leg power (over-bending) in free throw shooting; just that slight initial knee flexion, combined with an efficient foot push should allow you to produce fluid rhythm. On the contrary, if your legs are too straight and stiff, you will create a tense momentum that will not transfer smoothly to your upper body, thus producing a choppy rhythm, tense release and hard shot on the rim.

Figure 3.3 *Leg motion.*

ARM MOTION

In order to create good rhythm, your upper body movements must be in synch with the lower body's initial loading process. Your arm's swinging motion must complement the leg motion to produce more momentum, force and rhythm during the shot. As your legs begin to extend, you start the arm action of transferring the ball from your initial shooting pocket position to your release point (the two key ball positions), and then finish the shot with a good follow-through.

Figure 3.4 *Arm motion.*

THE TWO KEY BALL POSITIONS

Figure 3.5 *Shooting pocket.*

Figure 3.6 *Release point.*

1. Shooting Pocket

Coaches have different theories regarding where a correct shot should begin, but you have to determine what feels most comfortable to you and from where you can produce the smoothest motion and force to release the ball. This initial ball position is called the shooting pocket. Although every player may prefer a lower or higher pocket, depending on body structure, size, strength or age, ideally you should hold the ball in the stomach-chest area, below your shoulders, on your strong side (right if right-handed, left if left-handed) just like in your classic triple-threat basketball stance. As we discussed in Chapter 2, maintaining a balanced and compact foundation (keeping elbows near hips) will allow you to minimize arm movements and raise the ball efficiently to the next position: your release point.

2. Release Point

The other key ball position is your release point. This position is not where the ball is released from the fingers, but the area to which you raise the ball from your shot pocket, just before the full extension of the shooting arm. Like with the shooting pocket, your body structure, arm length, and strength, make this position a bit subjective and you may be forced to make a natural adaptation. The ideal release point is right above the eye/forehead area on your strong side: somewhere between the eye and ear, in order to allow the best alignment possible with the basket. Your ball position must enable you to see the rim properly (shooting window), so that you don't have to change your head position, which can compromise your shooting alignment. An incorrect release point can negatively affect your rhythm, momentum, view, form and, of course, accuracy.

Elbow Lift – The elbow lift determines the height of your release point. This position should depend on your body structure and strength:

1. Quarter Lift: ball at chin level – often smaller or weaker players.
2. Half Lift: ball above eye – 90-degree angles, most correct technique.
3. Three Quarter Lift: ball above head – often taller or longer-armed players.

Whether you have a high or low release point, what matters most is that your elbow remains "in", aligned with the goal, allowing maximum power.

FOUR TECHNICAL MISCONCEPTIONS RELATED TO SHOOTING RHYTHM

1. **"MORE LEGS" THEORY** - Stressing "more legs" at the free throw line is not always the best advice. Proper leg use is an important factor in basketball, as it allows you to establish stable foundation and balance, and also initi-

Figure 3.7 *Quarter lift*

Figure 3.8 *Half lift.*

Figure 3.9 *Three Quarter lift.*

Figure 3.10 *An exaggerated knee flexion is unnecessary and may add tension in the lower body.*

ate the process for a smooth shot motion. But I wouldn't go any further when it comes to free throw shooting. Too often I hear a coach yell at his player after a missed first foul shot "more legs"! What does that mean, especially when the shot was missed to the right or left? Proper leg bend allows you to create rhythm in your shot, but LEGS DON'T MAKE BASKETS! Especially at the free throw line. While with very young kids, extra leg power may help them reach the rim, with teenage and adult players I strongly discourage excessive leg flexion during a free throw routine as it may cause too much tension in the lower body that eventually may not allow an efficient force transfer to the upper body.

2. **ELIMINATING EXCESS MOTION** - We opened the Mechanics chapter addressing how important it is to establish a strong balanced base and compact position, holding the ball close to your body in order to reduce excessive movement that can raise your chances for error in the shot motion. In shooting rhythm this is extremely important in order to maximize positive forces throughout the body. You want to have an economy of motion, but not at the cost of damaging your shooting rhythm, since it is a key factor in free throw shooting. In an attempt to eliminate any wasted movements and to compact their free throw shot in order to lower any chance for error, many big players unfortunately cut out their foot and leg motions. While reducing excess movement is a valid concept, sometimes taller players make the mistake of totally eliminating that little knee bend (even just a few degrees) and foot push that initiates rhythm throughout the body. The results are tense releases, and hard misses on the rim. Even just a minimum degree of knee flexion can help generate that little push of positive energy that will travel throughout your entire body into the release of the ball. Your initial leg bend and foot push are crucial factors at the foul line. If eliminating movements

RAY ALLEN'S "STIFF" FREE THROW TECHNIQUE

There have been cases of successful "stiff" foul shooters. A primary example is Ray Allen, who uses very little if any leg power at the line. As much as I love his game and shooting ability, I do not like or recommend his free throw technique... but at 90 percent, I would not have much to say to him about it!

means reducing shooting rhythm, then you need to review your technique/motion and perhaps tweak another loose part.

3. **HIGH SHOT POCKET** - One of the biggest misconceptions in shooting is that you should begin your shot high because it is quicker, harder to block and requires less arm movement. I understand the theoretic concept, but if you try this method, you will realize that you create very little momentum and shot rhythm, which in real game situations translates into limited shooting range. Not to mention that by holding the ball in your shoulder/chin area, your one-on-one game will be extremely limited as you are no longer a threat to attack off the dribble. Unless the player is big and extremely strong, it is rare to see a successful shot technique that begins with a high shot pocket. In a static shot like the free throw, where you must create your rhythm with your feet still, there is no doubt that a standard stomach-chest area shot pocket allows the smoothest motion and best results.

LOW SHOT POCKET TECHNIQUES

I can think of very few successfully smooth free throw shooters with a high shot pocket, and usually they are taller and/or stronger players. One is former NBA great Rolando Blackman, a terrific shooter at 6-6, who began his foul shot at chin level. Another is 6-7 Klay Thompson of the Golden State Warriors, who begins at chest level. Many of the NBA's best shooters today, including Steve Nash, Steph Curry, Damien Lillard, and Kyrie Irving, have very low shot techniques that produce an effortless stroke.

Figure 3.11 *A high release point can hurt your shooting rhythm.*

4. **HIGH RELEASE POINT** - This is another misconception. If you are a seven-footer with long arms, it will be natural to raise the ball higher above your head or even a bit behind it. But, in general, players with this technique are neither smooth shooters nor accurate shot makers. Releasing the ball too high above your head can cause several problems: a tense upper body, possible negative motion, or a hitch or hesitation at the top of your motion, as your arm movement will not get the most out of the extension. All these issues will cause you to lose or damage your shot rhythm, which will result in a tense release and hard ball on the rim.

KYLE KORVER'S IMPROVEMENTS

In a 2015 "USA Today" article covering his amazing NBA-leading shooting percentages, Kyle Korver explains how his improvements were achieved more through proper attention to his physical aspects than actual shooting technique. By addressing his postural and muscular deficiencies, he was able to understand his body components better in order to find his rhythm and improve his overall percentages.

STABILIZING THE LEG AND ARM MOTIONS TO MAXIMIZE RHYTHM: THE IMPORTANCE OF CORE STRENGTH

In shooting, there is an underrated and often neglected physical component that comes into play, even at the free throw line, which is your core strength. There are primary and secondary muscles which contract in order to deliver the shot. You must avoid that the non-shooting muscles interfere as they can add unwanted tension to the motion which can chop up your rhythm. Your core musculature becomes of critical importance in stabilizing the shot, as your abdominal and lower back muscles contract isometrically to support your primary movers. Your core is defined by your body's mid-section, and all the muscles that attach to the hips, pelvis and spine. The core plays an important role in sports as it is the place where all movements begin and where the body's center of gravity is located. In free throw shooting, core strength becomes essential for the power transfer from the lower body to upper body, which generates shooting rhythm. As we've discussed, a good shot technique depends on leg power and arm power to produce the necessary force for the shot motion. The legs would not be able to transfer the power efficiently to the arms if your core didn't stabilize the force transfer, and your rhythm would be weak. With an unstable or weak mid-section, only a small amount of the force generated by your legs will reach your arms, and your shot's rhythm will be choppy or weak. This is a key concept in order to develop a consistent shooting technique, not only in free throws, but also jump shooting and long range shooting.

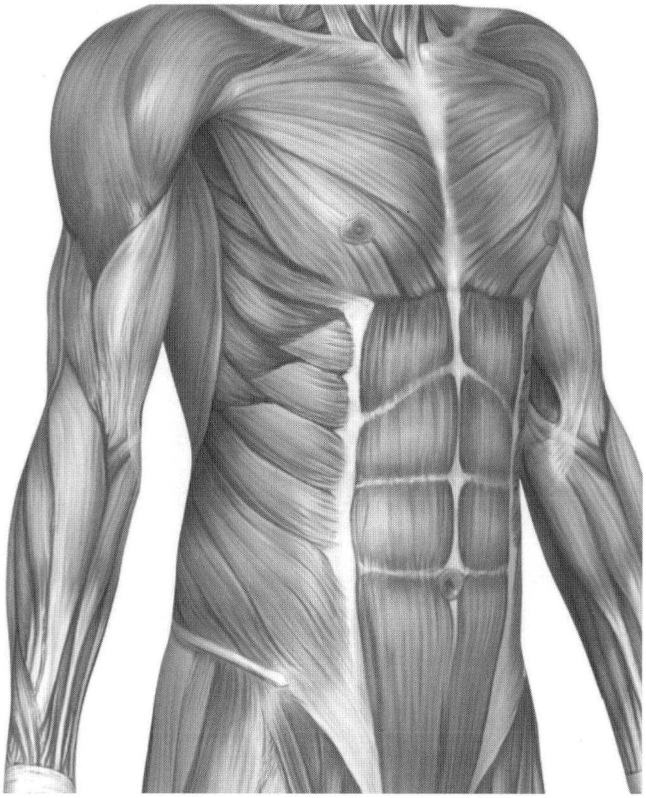

Figure 3.12 *The body's core musculature is key in stabilizing the shot.*

In order to shoot the ball consistently over and over through fatigue, you want to get the most out of the least amount of effort. Your free throw stroke should be effortless with no strain. Activating the core muscles will relax your upper body, as it reduces the tension in your arms, shoulders and neck. Personally, training and strengthening my core over the past few years has helped to smooth out my shot rhythm and allowed me to shoot for longer stretches without getting tired.

UNDERSTANDING NEGATIVE MOTION (Backward Force)

SHOT DIRECTION
Negative movements take you away from the basket

Figure 3.13 *Negative motion.*

I refer to all the body's and ball's movements that lead toward the basket as "positive", and all the ones that push you in the opposite direction, away from the rim, as "negative". Typically, negative motions have to do with improper movements of the shoulders, head, heels and basketball itself. Examples:

- Leaning back.
- Retracting shoulders.
- Jerking your head back.
- Hopping back or fading.
- Not extending your feet so as to end on your toes, but falling back on your heels.
- Raising the ball too far behind your head.
- Cocking your wrist as you raise the ball instead of having it already in a "loaded" position as you catch it.
- Holding the ball too far out in front of your body, instead of close in your shooting pocket, within your foundation's cylinder. This will make you raise the ball with a backward force instead of an upward and forward force.
- Following the flight of the ball instead of keeping your eyes on the rim. This will make your head tilt back.

Figure 3.14 *Shoulder retraction and falling back on heels are the most common negative movements at the line.*

Figure 3.15 *Exposing the ball out of your cylinder can cause negative motion.*

Figure 3.16 *Raising the ball too far behind your head is a common negative movement.*

It often occurs that players, typically the bigger and more muscular ones, shoot the ball toward the goal, but somehow jerk backward so that the result is a tense force-struggle with the ball going one way and the player pulling back in the opposite direction. The brain gets lost in this power struggle. A very common example is what happens when a player's shoulders retract, pulling his heels back to the ground as the ball is being released. This usually leads to either a flat, short and/or hard shot that has neither rhythm nor touch to it.

In order to find fluid rhythm, I stress the importance of developing a body motion that follows the shot motion and ball trajectory. A straight "up and down" extension may be too stiff. Therefore, you should focus on extending your body with an upward and slightly forward motion, where you feel like your entire body is following the ball into the basket. That's why a positive foot extension is paramount in order to create a smooth, forceful but soft shooting technique.

WHAT IS A HITCH? HOW DO YOU FIX IT?

While it is more common in jump shooting, as players may tend to release the ball at the top of their jump, it is also possible to run into this technical flaw in free throw shooting. This issue is usually due to a prolonged pause at the release point before extending the shooting arm.

In order to get a clearer picture, let's break down the two synchronizations that occur during the mechanical motion:

1. Legs (knees) extend as arms raise the ball from the shot pocket to release point.
2. *Pause* – the motion pauses at your release point after having transferred the ball up from your shot pocket position.
3. Feet (ankles) extend (feet push off the ground giving force) as shooting arm extends and hand flexes, thrusting the ball.

The pause at the moment of release is the critical point of your shooting motion. The length and quality of this pause determines how fluid your extension will be. The briefer the pause at your release point, the smoother the rhythm and the quicker the shot. A prolonged pause or any sort of hesitation at your release point, kills momentum and erases all the positive force implemented up to this point. The result is a hitch, which causes a choppy shot rhythm.

Figure 3.17 *The pause at your release point must not interrupt your shot motion.*

Your motion should be so smooth and continuous that the pause barely occurs as you are relying more on a one-piece shot motion with no real stops throughout the movement. Focus on the extension process, don't interrupt the shot motion: all positive energy, upward and forward, toward the goal. I like to say "raise the ball *through* your release point, not to your release point", which emphasizes the sense of a single motion technique and fluidity.

The higher the release point, the higher the chances for a pause/hitch that can damage your rhythm. You want your upper body muscles to be relaxed: any head, neck and shoulder tension may cause you to jerk backward or to the side. Make sure that your body and head follow the trajectory of the ball *into* the goal.

FEET AND WRIST: THE SHOT'S TWO MOST UNDERRATED SOURCES OF POWER

When you begin feeling fatigue, you will search for additional power. At the free throw line, your resource for power does not necessarily come from bending your knees more than you typically do. Something I see every day, especially at the NBA level, is big strong players who miss free throws consistently "short". We have already listed several reasons why this occurs, but the fix is often a lot easier than you think.

In free throw shooting there are two underrated and usually underused forces: feet and wrist. At this distance, using more legs or exaggerating your knee flexion is usually not the right solution. Extending your feet and focusing on all the "positive" body movements is a huge source of power, which also helps create fluid rhythm. With efficient foot extension, your body will follow the ball with an upward and forward movement, so you should end up just very slightly forward with your chest, shoulders and head. Your shooting arm should extend as your heels leave the ground. Maintain your balance, activating your core muscles.

I encourage players to use a full wrist bend and a forceful, but not rigid, wrist snap that will send the ball straight to the goal. As we discussed when speaking about proper follow-through, the last part of the shot motion and last force implemented will affect the shot. So if you feel that your shot is a bit weak, compensate with a little extra wrist snap. Make sure it involves a smooth, not tense finger flexion: don't close your fingers too tightly as you extend the ball, as this will create a hard ball on the rim.

Figure 3.18 *Use an efficient foot extension.*

Figure 3.19 *Keep a loaded wrist at all times.*

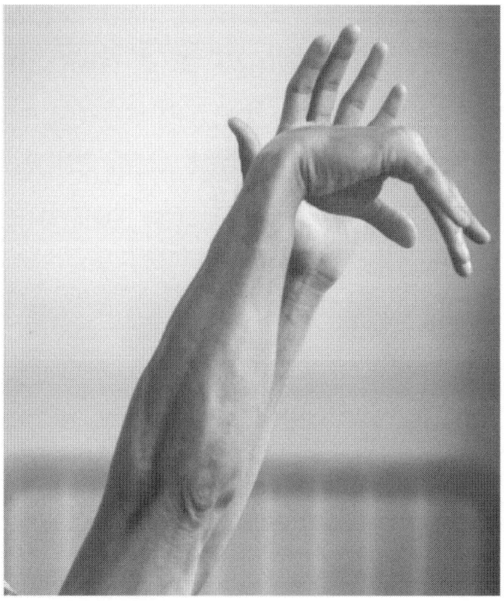

Figure 3.20 *Rely on a forceful, not tense, wrist snap.*

POSITIVE ENERGIES WORKING TOGETHER

Mastering the correct shot mechanics and understanding your body motion allows you to create shooting rhythm, which is synonymous with positive energy, coordination and effortless movement. That's what you want your body to feel during the free throw shot. The repetition of this rhythmic motion, combined with a positive mindset, allows muscle memory to make the process automatic and eventually second nature. No over-thinking, no effort, no tension, no hesitation, just swishes! You will develop a confident approach so that you will walk up to the line with positive energy every time you are fouled, and repeat the same positive habits, steps and thoughts that prove to work for you. By repeating the same process over and over, shot after shot, you will master an efficient free throw routine that makes you feel comfortable.

Figure 3.21 *Shooting rhythm.*

Chapter 4

CONTROLLING YOUR MIND: THE MENTAL SIDE

Controlling Your Mind: The Mental Side

"You play the game of basketball against yourself as much as against any opponent. It's mental as much as it is physical."

– Hall of Fame Player **Oscar Robertson**

How would you like walking up to the foul line knowing that you have already added the points to your stat line and your team's total even before you actually shoot the ball? Wouldn't that be great? Knowing that you are a great free throw shooter is huge, as you will step to the line focused and confident in your abilities. As a result, you will be a more aggressive 1 on 1 scorer, eager to get back to the line again for more easy points. Unfortunately you don't just wake up one day and have this kind of mindset and attitude. The entire process of consistent training, through dedication, self-discipline and a sense of pride, is what will enhance your concentration level and take you to that state of confidence.

Figure 4.1 *Focus, concentration, and confidence are key in free throw shooting.*

Focus and concentration, along with confidence, are the concepts that are most often associated with the mental side of free throw shooting. As important as they are, I feel there are some misconceptions, as these two alone will not allow you to make shots without a correct shooting form. Shooting technique is indeed the most important aspect in shooting success, but the mental side is the other key factor, and in no part of the game is it more important than at the free throw line. You may hear that the free throw shot is 50 percent technique and 50 percent mental, and although somewhat true, I prefer not to appoint a percentage to measure their importance, as they are both crucial to becoming a great free throw shooter. I personally consider the shot more mechanical than mental, but it's that amount of mental strength and confidence that can be the difference between an average free throw shooter and a great one. You can focus and believe in yourself as much as you want, but if you cannot shoot the ball with some sort of correct technique, you will not be able to make shots on a consistent basis regardless of the right mindset. As you progress to high level basketball, and have mastered proper shooting mechanics, the mental side will make all the difference in the world as it may be what is keeping you from becoming great.

FOCUS AND CONCENTRATION: STAY PLUGGED IN!

Although we often use them as synonyms, focus and concentration do have slightly different meanings. While in shooting I feel they work hand in hand, we should still distinguish between the two terms:

- **"Focus"** to me is a more specific action, in having a clear vision of what you are trying to accomplish: maintaining your attention in the moment, on the task at hand. In shooting this means not thinking about the past (especially bad experiences like a previous 0-2 with the game on the line) and the future ("will I make or miss?" thoughts).
- **"Concentration"** is a more general concept in my opinion. In free throw shooting, concentrating better doesn't mean to stare at the rim or try harder at putting the ball in the hoop! In very basic terms, to me concentration is the ability to eliminate outside distractions, controlling your thoughts and emotions.

However you view the two concepts in terms of shooting free throws, both focus and concentration need to be disciplined. I am neither a psychiatrist nor a mental trainer, but one thing I have learned is that going through the process of mastering the skill of shooting, disciplining yourself every day, and training the right way, will help you develop and/or improve your shooting concentration: especially with free throws since you are repeating the exact same motion from the exact same spot every time. Great free throw shooters block out all outside distractions and focus on what they can control: the correct mechanics that allow them to make the shot.

There is also a strong physical component to maintaining focus and concentration throughout an entire basketball game or practice. Good training habits will not only improve your technique and attention span, but also better your stamina, endurance, and general physical conditioning. To be a consistent shot maker, especially at the free throw line, you rely on the consistency of your brain and your body. As you begin to feel fatigued, your concentration will also begin to drop. Therefore, if both your body and your brain start to drift, so will your shot.

MIND DRIFTING

Mind drifting is a term that describes what may happen to a shooter who is not able to maintain concentration at the free throw line for a long period of time during practice. Usually this has to do with either fatigue, boredom or disinterest in what you are doing. In real games, only fatigue should be able to occur, as having just one, two or three shots at your disposal, it's hard to be bored... and if you are disinterested then you do not belong on the team. However, in a practice setting all three conditions can come into play to disrupt your shooting performance: you may be tired after a stressful workout or team practice, you may become superficial in your approach while shooting a large number of shots at once, or you would simply prefer being elsewhere. Always focus on one shot at a time, and eliminate all distractions.

"One important key to success is self-confidence. An important key to self-confidence is preparation."

– Tennis Legend **Arthur Ashe**

CONFIDENCE

Confident free throw shooters believe in themselves and have a positive approach: they trust their shooting technique and free throw routine, don't doubt themselves, know they will make the shot. With that being said, it would be silly and unrealistic for me to tell a player "always believe in yourself" or "stay positive" when he or she may never have experienced any tangible results, let alone success. Saying you are confident when you cannot make a shot is just an in-denial and unrealistic statement. How can you be confident or optimistic if you have not seen the ball go in consistently? Remember there is no luck at the free throw line: either you can shoot the ball or not. You can't just decide to be confident all of a sudden, you have to "earn" confidence.

"Lack of confidence is born from a lack of preparation."

– **Shannon Wilburn**

PRACTICE IS YOUR WORKSHOP

In shooting the basketball, confidence is built through the training process of learning, perfecting and mastering the fundamental mechanics of a correct shot technique. It's the hours of practice and repetition, through self-discipline and dedication, topped with successful results, that allows you to "earn" confidence. So instead of "believing in yourself" you should be more focused on "believing in the hours of practice you put in to master that smooth shooting technique".

In order to develop confidence in your shooting technique, you must see results or at least glimpses of success to understand what

PRACTICE RESULTS

Success in practice should not be underrated, as it is a big step toward mastering the free throw. I often hear people say "let's see if you can make free throws in games", and there is no doubt that game pressure makes the task of converting free throws more difficult. While there are players who are not able to transfer their practice success into games, I know for sure that those who can make free throw shots in games are all outstanding shooters in practice. So if you want to be great in game conditions, you must first become great in practice conditions!

confidence feels like. Failing over and over or not preparing at all, you will only know what insecurity and doubt are. This is why practice and repetition are so important. You need to see the ball go through the net to believe in what you are doing and have a positive mindset. That's why I begin every workout with my routine of basic technique warmup shots close to the basket, working myself back only as I see the ball go in consistently. This way my mind sees the rim get bigger and wider as I move farther away, and I begin to expect to make every shot. Only after this basic daily exercise do I progress into jump shooting and long distance shots.

If you are not committed to practice or have a superficial approach, whether you are a player or the team's coach, you cannot expect to see any sort of confidence at game time, not to mention when you are at the line with two shots to tie or win the game. In order to have success in games at the free throw line, you must see results in practice first. Practice is where you develop proper technique and begin feeling good about yourself. Through practice results you get a feel for what success tastes like, and once you transfer this state of mind to the game and establish yourself as a great free throw shooter, you will feel confident in your abilities.

Some players may have mastered the free throw and are beginning to see results, but something is missing in terms of mental reassurance as they may have not had the opportunity to test themselves yet in game conditions. Whether because of lack of playing time, or not many trips to the foul line and not in pressure situations, maybe confidence has been a bit "dormant". Often it is a successful experience that triggers or unleashes your confidence. Hitting two game winning free throws as a kid was the key event that changed my mental approach and powered my confidence at the line. Finding out that you can do something is a big confidence boost, and makes you believe in the practice process you have committed to.

BREAKING IN A NEW TECHNIQUE

Making a change in your shooting form is never easy, but is often necessary for you to improve: in fact, sometimes you need to take a step back in order to eventually take one forward. Any major mechanical adjustment or even a little tweak will probably have you thinking "this doesn't feel right" at some point and you may begin doubting the process. Don't lose your confidence! Stay with it! You must have patience, and should not get discouraged. It's just like breaking in a new pair of shoes: initially they may feel uncomfortable, but the more you use them the better they feel. Give it some time, successful results are coming!

BODY LANGUAGE

All great shooters have that "swagger" as confidence travels throughout their mind and entire body. You can see this in their body language: they are focused, calm, determined and step to the line carrying themselves as if they knew they were the best shooters in the building regardless of whether they are in fact or not. Being confident doesn't mean being arrogant and talking trash to your opponents or teammates. It's knowing you know how to do something effectively.

Confidence leads to positive thinking. As you gain confidence in your shooting ability, you become more positive in your thought process at the line: you see yourself making each shot, do not get discouraged, do not doubt yourself, the idea of missing never crosses your mind. Most of all, you have the ability to instantly erase a mistake and believe you will make the next shot!

The more shots you make, the more confident you get! There is a thin line between confident and cocky, so don't let overconfidence lead you to presumption, which at some point will backfire as you might think you don't need to train anymore. Great shooters constantly renew their confidence through good practice habits and repetition, challenging themselves every day.

PRACTICE IS KEY IN DEVELOPING CONFIDENCE, BUT ALSO IN MAINTAINING IT: THE CYCLE OF SUCCESS

Once you reach a high level of confidence, remember that it is not permanent, because success is not permanent. You need to constantly renew your confidence through consistent practice so you can experience more successful results. As obsessive as this sounds, this is the cycle of success that pushes great players to reach their highest capabilities. Work ethic and dedication to individual practice will lead you to repeating the correct shot motion and technique, which will become ingrained in your muscle memory. Your shooting percentages will improve and your confidence level will rise.

The new mindset will transfer to your game shots and one-on-one game as you will be more aggressive attacking the basket. Successful results breed confidence in your abilities. Confidence makes you believe in the practice process and pushes you to return to the gym to renew your confidence over and over. It's a beautiful cycle, which builds a winning mentality.

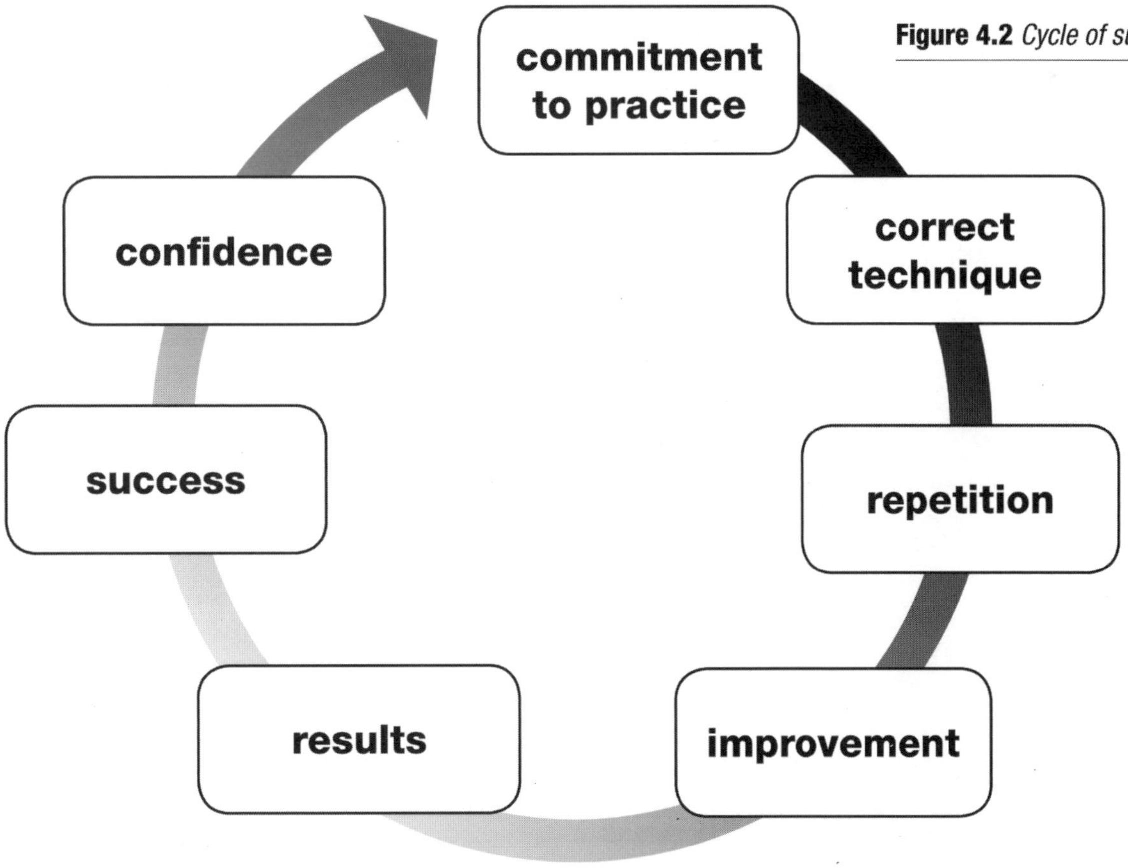

Figure 4.2 *Cycle of success.*

MENTAL REASSURANCE

Everyone, even the best shooters, need reassurance at times. Whether it's during the learning process or an actual game when you just missed a shot, during a training session or when you are in a temporary shooting slump, at some point everyone needs a little reassurance. Relying on others can comfort you, but your confidence depends on you! Here are seven key reassurance points to remember during your journey in mastering the free throw shot, that should reassure you and keep your mindset positive at all times:

1. **THE GOAL IS BIG** - Let's go back to the tools of the game of basketball for a moment. The goal is big and it doesn't move. The ball's size is much smaller, its diameter being almost exactly half that of the rim, and almost three basketballs can actually fit within the circumference. Since the rim is 18 inches in diameter and the ball is approximately 9, this means there is a 4 ½ inch margin for error all around the rim. For younger kids and women, using a smaller ball, the ball to rim circumference ratio is even larger.

Figure 4.3 *The rim's diameter is twice that of the basketball.*

2. **YOU IMPROVE JUST BY REDUCING CHANCES OF ERROR** - Another key reassurance aspect lies within the concept of "shooting the ball straight". This is the first thing I stress when I begin working with a player because of its inherent simplicity: if you learn how to shoot the ball straight, thus eliminating potential right and left missed shots, you are also reducing your chances of error. Short and long misses are easier to adjust, and in any case, they indicate your mechanics are in line.

Figure 4.4 *By learning to shoot the ball straight you are reducing chances of error.*

3. **THE PERFECT SHOT IS AN IDEAL** - Ideally you would like to shoot a picture perfect shot which goes through the rim with an all net "swish" every time you are at the free throw line. It's a beautiful image and feeling, but striving for perfection can often add unwanted tension and pressure. You don't want to get frustrated if every shot does not go in as cleanly as you would like. Sometimes you have to simply "settle" for a made free throw and not an ideal picture perfect one! Knowing that even a not-so-perfect shot still counts is big in terms of mental reassurance.

PERSONAL EXPERIENCE

I wish I could say that I swish every shot straight through the middle of the rim; or shoot with the exact same release every time; but I don't as it is virtually impossible to do, especially when you are shooting for long stretches. However, because my basic mechanics are correct, it does reassure me to know that even if my release is slightly off at times, there is still a good chance the ball will go in. As long as my shot line is centered between the two sides of the rim and my elbow extends at/above eye level, I know I am giving the right coordinates for a successful shot... swish or not.

4. **EVEN THE BEST SHOOTERS MISS SHOTS** - Another reassuring fact is knowing that even the best players and shooters miss shots, including free throws from time to time. I have been lucky to be around the NBA for many years, and have watched professional players play, practice, train and warm-up countless times. Even if you idolize these NBA stars and look at them as immortal, guess what? They are human, which means they have both good and bad days, lose focus at times, get tired and frustrated, and not only do they not swish every shot, they also miss shots! It's what they do with their misses that matters! Don't get discouraged and hit the next shot! The next shot is always the most important one!

> *"What to do with a mistake: recognize it, admit it, learn from it, forget it."*
>
> – Hall of Fame Coach **Dean Smith**

5. **MISSED SHOTS ARE NECESSARY IN ORDER TO GROW** - Mistakes are your form of discovery: you need to make errors in order to improve, as learning to analyze and instantly correct will allow you to reach that next level. Accept missed shots as part of the learning process of mastering the free throw shot. In order to progress and become an elite shooter, mistakes are necessary, they are your "fertilizer". Misses allow you to learn how to recognize the reasons for errors, so that you can make self-adjustments and achieve your ultimate goal of learning how to coach yourself.

6. **GAME PERCENTAGES ARE ALWAYS LOWER THAN PRACTICE PERCENTAGES** - It's normal that your game shooting percentages are not as high as your practice numbers. You may not get to the foul line often, you may get fouled when you have just entered the game and are still a bit "cold". You normally only have 1 or 2 shots so it is harder to find your stroke or make progressive adjustments like in practice. It's the same shot, but the circumstances and surroundings are different. In any case, if you master proper technique and develop great confidence, even if you do not make every free throw in real games, you should still be able to maintain a good percentage.

7. **YOU MAY BE BETTER THAN WHAT YOU THINK YOU ARE** - Many players are far better free throw shooters than what they think... they just don't know it yet! Your own preconceived beliefs may be what has imprisoned your confidence and limited your per-

formance so far. By underestimating your abilities, you are unconsciously either content with mediocre results or are convinced that you cannot improve... or probably both. If you consider 70 percent to be an elite level or think it is the best you can do, maybe you have not pushed or challenged yourself enough in order to breed your potential confidence: you may be closer to being a 90 percent foul shooter than you think. Don't ever stop at your assumed limitations: you will be surprised how far you can go when you put your mind to it!

"Don't measure yourself by what you have accomplished, but by what you should have accomplished with your ability."

– Hall of Fame Coach and Player
John Wooden

STUDIES AND EXPERIMENTS IN MENTAL TRAINING

Over the years there have been countless studies related to mental visualization in sports. A particular experiment specifically involving free throw shooting was conducted on more than one occasion. It involved three groups of players who were given different instructions, and then tested for improvement after a period of thirty days. The first group was instructed to practice free throws every day; the second group was told to simply visualize themselves shooting successful free throws during that time; the third group was asked to do nothing, no practice and no visualization. The results were amazing: while it was no surprise that the third group showed no improvements, the amount of progress of the visualizing group was very close to the improvements of the first group that had consistently practiced their free throws on a daily basis.

MENTAL IMAGERY/VISUALIZATION

When I was a high school player, my head coach tried getting the team to meditate and practice visualization. The result was half the team goofing off and the other half falling asleep (I managed doing a bit of both). The topic of mental imagery or visualization in sports performance can be delicate and intimidating as it is a subjective one, so I am sure you will find plenty of doubters out there. I myself have always been very skeptical about a lot of methods I read or hear about. But my perspective has drastically changed after experimenting first hand and seeing the results. While I cannot estimate or quantify the improvements I have experienced, I can definitely say that mental imagery is an extremely powerful technique and tool in sports, especially in free throw shooting. While I am neither a mental trainer nor a sports psychologist, I have always been a big dreamer who is in love with the game. As childish as it sounds, fantasizing about making a smooth picture perfect game-winning shot can be an extremely efficient mental practice that can lead to amazing results. Numerous athletes in various sports, from basketball to tennis, from golf to baseball, in one way or another are adopting the technique of mental imagery for personal development and to achieve their specific goals. Free throw shooting is perhaps the best example in any sport of a task that can be improved through mental training.

But what exactly is mental imagery? How does it work? A common definition of mental imagery is "the human ability to visualize images in our minds after the original stimuli is out of view". Although the terms may be slightly different, mental imagery, visualization, or mental rehearsal are mind training techniques that involve practicing a skill or action in your mind through positive images.

Performing a specific skill like free throw shooting through mental imagery can help you improve your concentration and confidence levels, maintain a positive mindset and ability to stay in the moment (avoiding thoughts of the past and the future), control your emotions, enhance your sense of rhythm, and also help automize your shot mechanics: in fact, mental practice helps create neural patterns in your brain to develop muscle memory. In addition, this method can also help you prepare for your next performance.

PROPER SHOOTING TECHNIQUE

You cannot expect to see measurable results using mental training methods without already having a correct shooting technique. Mental imagery is simply not as valuable without proper shooting mechanics. However, combining it with a good shooting form, visualization becomes a major tool to enhance both concentration and confidence.

Basketball is a game for creative people. Mental imagery requires that you imagine yourself in the typical game environment performing a free throw shot using all of your senses: sight, sound, and feel. A player who has experienced the actual feelings and emotions involved can understand. The images you recreate in your mind must be of you performing the shot successfully and feeling good (comfortable and confident) about your shot motion.

There is no correct way in mental training. You can practice mental imagery for a brief duration or long duration; can use it before competition, during competition, after competition. You should rely on visualization in practice and games, every time before you execute a free throw shot. See and feel yourself going through the shot motion in your mind, with a smooth release and confident follow-through, and visualize the ball falling through the center of the rim with a perfect swish!

There are two types of mental imagery: one is first-person imagery, which is called "internal"; the other is third-person imagery, which is called "external". Both methods can be very effective in different ways:

1. **FIRST-PERSON / INTERNAL IMAGERY:** This method, which supposedly produces the best results, consists of recreating the setting in your mind, putting yourself at the foul line and visualizing the situation through your own eyes as you go through your shot routine. You need to imagine yourself performing the shot, just as you do during an actual free throw. Focus on involving all of your senses: sight, sound and feel. See the rim in front of you and the ball in your hands; see your hands held up as you freeze your follow-through and the ball about to fall through the basket. Hear the sound of your dribble and wrist/finger flexion as you release the ball, the noise of the fans and the swishing of the net. Feel the ball in your hands, feel your body in rhythm. Make sure you incorporate your typical breathing pattern also to make ev-

erything as realistic as possible. Internal mental imagery, like meditation, is not an easy exercise as it takes a lot of concentration to recreate the typical setting and execution of a mental free throw.

2. **THIRD-PERSON / EXTERNAL IMAGERY:** This is a slightly different mental exercise as you are now seeing yourself through the eyes of a spectator. You are basically watching yourself from a distance, so you need to visualize your entire body going through the shot motion. With external mental imagery there are less benefits than first-person visualization, as it is harder to focus on your senses and feelings with this method. However, what I like about this method is that you can recreate this exercise in the form of video.

VISUALIZATION AND VIDEO

Even if third-person (external) imagery is supposedly not as beneficial, if you combine it with video it becomes a powerful exercise. You can either film yourself practicing and create a brief video of a successful shooting sequence where you felt in rhythm, or you can edit a short clip of made shots from official game video. Watching yourself make shots and re-living that sensation of confidence or being in a "zone", can be yet another positive reinforcement exercise, that can help raise performance. Do it on a daily basis. The video clip can be 1 to 5 minutes long, with 10 to 50 shots. As you gather new video with more successful shooting streaks, create newer and better clips to add to your file and always keep them handy on your phone or tablet.

PERSONAL EXPERIENCE

Video is an extremely powerful tool! I discovered it a bit too late, but it has been of fundamental importance to me in recent years for analyzing both the players and myself! Not only does it help you see any flaws in your shooting technique, but it also reassures you of what you are doing correctly. Seeing yourself do something consistently well makes you expect to continue doing it well. Watching video of yourself shooting the ball successfully represents third-person (external) imagery that can be an additional training method that leads to improved performance. Reviewing clips of successful shooting streaks, converting shot after shot with flawless form, is extremely constructive in the process of building confidence and a positive approach.

COMBINING VISUALIZATION WITH THE CONCEPT OF TARGET / AIMING POINT AT THE FREE THROW LINE

In our Mechanics section we introduced the subject of mental imagery and visualization while addressing target and aiming point. The idea of visualizing the perfect image of a perfect shot is a key factor in shooting the basketball, but most specifically in free throw shooting.

At the foul line, as soon as I locate the rim and am about to begin the extension motion, I see the image of a perfect shot: the ball exactly above the goal about to drop through it with a perfect swish. This part of the process is one of the most important steps of an efficient free throw routine as it automatically gives you your "aiming point", or where you want to direct the ball. Most of all, the mental picture of a successful shot is a "positive" image that rein-

Figure 4.5
Mental visualization of a perfect shot.

forces confidence and allows for better focus.

In addition, combining the concept of aiming point through visualization with repetitive free throw practice, also has a strong effect on your basic shooting mechanics as you are reinforcing the idea of shooting the ball straight, developing muscle memory for a straight shot.

Think less, visualize more!

Research shows that our minds work well with images. Mental imagery helps you stay away from that possible "over-thinking" state of mind, where you are trying too hard to make the shot and doubling the pressure in your head. Focusing on a mental picture alleviates the pressure of making the shot, and gives you a sense of reassurance and relaxation (don't forget to take a deep breath before visualizing the perfect image).

Always end your practice session on a perfect free throw shot. It's not enough to finish with two or more made shots. The mental image of that last converted shot is what you want to carry over to the next day or upcoming game: that feeling, that image, that confidence!

THE THOUGHT PROCESS

Great free throw shooters have practiced the correct mechanics to exhaustion and have automized their technique, so they now can rely on muscle memory and do not need to think much about what they are doing. They are used to seeing the ball going in, and expect to see the ball go in on every shot. However, a younger and inexperienced player, or a low percentage shooter, needs some direction.

What should you think about and focus on when you are at the free throw line? I hear players give all kinds of answers like: "making the shot", "nothing", "not missing", "shooting straight", "other stuff" etc. While I don't know if there is a correct answer, any negative thoughts are obviously not good, so you have to train your brain to stay away from anything that may lead to a negative mindset or thought process. Understanding what to think about, or better yet what NOT to think about, is crucial at the line, and it takes time and experience to figure out what works best for you. A positive mindset at the free throw line involves a combination of things we have addressed or will be talking about in this section and the following chapter, such as: concentration, confidence, picturing a successful shot in your mind, the ability to keep your focus on the moment, stressing a key mechanical component, and putting everything together in the form of an efficient free throw routine.

Basketball is a dynamic, energetic, creative and instinctive game, which is mostly played with your unconscious mind because of the fast pace at which it is played. In a static setting like the free throw shot, where you have time to think, your conscious mind may work its way back into play and try to disrupt your instinctive muscle memory actions. Muscle memory and instincts are, in fact, what best represent your unconscious mind, while thinking, analyzing, processing have more to do with your conscious mind.

Your conscious mind is too slow to keep up with the speed of the game of basketball, as it can only process a few things at a time. It is impossible to perform with an active conscious mind as your reactions would be too slow and you would move like a robot. A negative mindset, whether by over-thinking or over-analyzing the situation (score, importance of shot, etc.), is often the result of your conscious mind taking over at the free throw line. This is why adopting a free throw routine and repeating it each time you step to the line is so important, as you will rely on an automatic step by step ritual to guide you through each shot.

Although your conscious mind should remain passive during competition, it is key during the learning process in your practice setting as it allows you to focus on specific details. When listening, observing, analyzing, and learning a new skill or correcting a mechanical shooting part, it is your conscious mind that is more active as it is better at assimilating all the information your brain needs in order to master proper technique. Through repetition and constant practice your shooting mechanics will become more second nature, automatic and instinctive, transitioning from the conscious to the unconscious side.

Focus, concentration, confidence and adopting an efficient free throw routine are what allows you to stay in the zone, and avoid falling into the conscious over-thinking/over-analyzing negative mindset that leads to choking at the foul line.

INSTINCTS (UNCONSCIOUS) VS THINKING (CONSCIOUS)

UNCONSCIOUS MIND	CONSCIOUS MIND
• **Muscle Memory**	• **Thinking**
• **Instincts**	• **Analysis**
• **Creativity**	• **Observation**
• **Game speed**	• **Learning**
• **Focus on the whole picture**	• **Focus on details**
• **Is aware of more things at once**	• **Processes only 1-2 things at once**

"Don't think too much. You'll create a problem that wasn't even there in the first place."

– Unknown

STAY IN THE MOMENT!

Being able to focus on the moment is a major mental point in shooting a successful free throw. The game of basketball is played in the moment, not in the past and not in the future; therefore you must forbid your mind from traveling both in the past and the future, as your thoughts may lead to anxiety, tension, hesitation, or impatience. Never leave the NOW, don't jump to the future and the idea of the outcome of the shot or the game, or worse yet, take yourself back to a negative experience where perhaps you missed two crucial free throws.

Focus on the moment and on YOU. At the free throw line only you are in control, so you must focus on what only you can control, and that's your shot technique and free throw routine. You can't allow yourself to worry about the score, the time on the clock, the fans, the opponents and the importance of the next shot.

Both in game situations and in a practice setting, you cannot think about your goal at the free throw line: whether it's hitting 2-2 in the game or 50-50 in practice, you cannot be driven by accomplishing a specific goal, because goals live in the future not the present. Setting goals is positive for motivation, but do not bring them into the competition with you. Never put too much emphasis on the outcome of the shot or on your goal. The next shot is always the most important one: stay in the moment, focus on one shot at a time, and always visualize a successful shot. Your mindset should not be about converting 100

PERSONAL EXPERIENCE

Since I always practice a large amount of free throws at once (not always recommended), usually with specific goals in mind, my concentration is challenged. Unlike shooting just two shots at a time, my mind tends to drift and lose focus on the moment. It takes patience as it's very easy to fall into the trap of time traveling, thinking more about the goal, with thoughts like "I have just 20 shots left" or "I have to make 100 in a row" rather than just "the next shot". Concentrate on one free throw at a time, not the goal: focus on the journey, not the destination.

PHIL JACKSON'S "FOCUS ON THE JOURNEY, NOT THE DESTINATION"

Hall of Fame Coach Phil Jackson, in his masterpiece book "Eleven Rings", talks about the challenges of his 1996-97 Chicago Bulls team early in the season. Coming off a championship year the team started the new season ready to play the finals right away as the players were too obsessed with their quest for another championship ring: their competitive nature was leading them to impatience too early in the year and the atmosphere was worrying Phil. His message to the team was to "focus on the journey rather than the destination": stay in the moment and enjoy the ride, do everything right during the process and at the end success will take care of itself.

In my opinion, Coach Jackson's philosophy applies to free throw shooting in many ways. It has, in fact, had a big impact on my mental approach and it accompanies me during my shooting instruction. You should not concentrate on your goal of making a free throw shot, rather take care of what needs to be done during the process. This is why a free throw routine is such a great method at the line: it allows you to focus on the right steps to guide you through the motion and not the thought of converting the actual shot and winning the game. This mental approach applies to both each single free throw you attempt and specific practice goals where you may be trying to reach a number of made shots.

shots in a row, but rather just 1 shot... 100 times!

Too many players focus on success rather than the steps to reach success. It should be a "process over product" approach. A free throw routine is a great example of this performance concept. You focus on the steps of your routine, not thinking about making the shot and the importance of the shot.

EMPHASIZE KEY MECHANICAL COMPONENTS

At the free throw line you do not have enough time and, in any case, do not want to focus on too many things. You may rely on a mechanical reminder, either a trigger or reinforcement word that emphasizes a key fundamental of your technique. Typical terms that players focus on may be:

- **"LEGS"**: to assure you feel balance, stability and put force into the shot.
- **"STRAIGHT"**: as reinforcement to not allow any right or left misses.
- **"UP & FORWARD":** to focus on a smooth shot motion.
- **"ELBOW IN"**: to make sure you maintain proper alignment.
- **"FREEZE"**: as a reminder to finish your shot holding your follow-through.

Never focus on more than one or two mechanical parts, and most of all do not start analyzing them. You repeat these words (always 1 term, not a bunch of words) to either trigger, remind, or reinforce. If you need to focus on two mechanical issues, repeat the terms together, example "legs – freeze". Simple terms, simple thoughts.

ADOPT A FREE THROW ROUTINE

Adopting a free throw routine gives you something to think about and focus on in the moment, rather than falling into time traveling or negative self talk. While we will go more in depth in the next chapter, I felt it necessary to introduce the concept of a routine now as it is of great importance in order to approach the free throw shot with a positive mindset. Going through the same ritual at the line every time, allows you to both relax and focus on something other than the outcome of the shot, thus relieving the unnecessary pressure. Your preparation may involve taking, let's say, three dribbles, gripping the ball with your fingers positioned correctly, taking a deep breath, visualizing a made shot and holding your follow-through. Each step of the routine automatically promotes a key mechanical component of your shot motion. With time and increased confidence, your free throw routine becomes second nature and automatic, as you will go through the steps as easy as 1-2-3 or A-B-C, and shoot. Same ritual every time! In the next chapter you will learn how to develop your own personal routine, that stresses proper technique, positive thoughts, consistency... and successful results!

STAY OFF THE LINE

Stay off the line until the rest of the players set up and the referee is ready to hand you the ball. Waiting too long on the line can lead to anxiety or impatience, and cause you to think more about the shot you are about to attempt.

NO DOUBTS, NO HESITATION

Once you have positioned the ball correctly in your hands while in your foundation stance, there should be no further adjustments. Changing hand or finger position on the ball as you begin the shot motion is a sign of insecurity and hesitation. Always keep a stable (not tense) grip on the ball. Visualize the perfect shot. Take a deep breath to relax, and begin the extension sequence with decision and

Figure 4.6 *Keep a stable grip on the ball.*

confidence. No "alligator arm" (timid, choppy or partial extension), extend and finish, freezing your follow-through with your shooting fingers "inside the rim".

NEGATIVE MINDSET

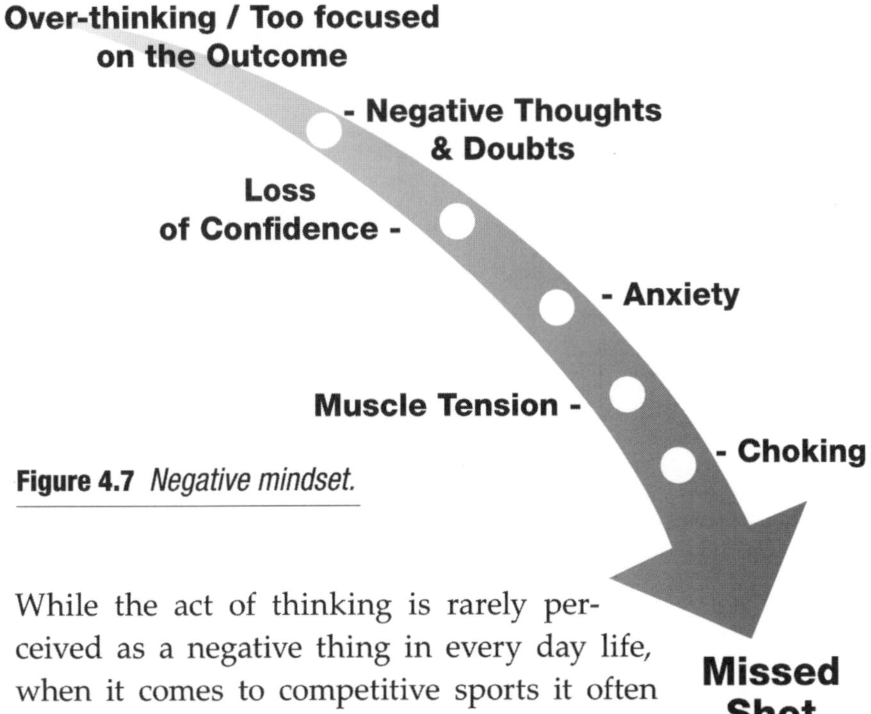

Figure 4.7 *Negative mindset.*

While the act of thinking is rarely perceived as a negative thing in every day life, when it comes to competitive sports it often is. In an instinctive game like basketball, it will slow down your reactions and lead you to making mistakes. In free throw shooting things get worse! A negative mindset at the line is the result of too much thinking and/or focusing on the wrong things, which lead to negative thoughts involving the idea of missing and the importance of the shot: believing you cannot make the shot, visualizing a missed shot, past traumatic experiences, the aftermath of a possible miss, and fear of disappointing yourself and other people. Thinking, or trying too hard to make a free throw shot, leads you to a state of doubt, hesitation, anxiety and

FEELING PRESSURE

Feeling a little pressure is normal, and actually a good thing as it helps you to focus better. But, never allow common pressure to lead to negative thoughts or anxiety will prevent you from having a clear mind.

PERSONALIZED WORDS AND PHRASES

It is common for players to use personalized key words as either mechanical reminders, reinforcement or mental reassurance during their free throw motion. Another method, used when negative thoughts try to take over, involves "pattern breaking" words or phrases that you may say to yourself in order to re-transition to your usual positive mindset. Examples: "like every other time"; "just like in practice"; "one shot at a time"; "I know I'm a good shooter", etc.

tension, which is often referred to as "paralysis by analysis", or in basketball terms, "choking". With a negative mental approach you become your own opponent and you begin to see the rim smaller than ever.

FREE THROW SLUMPS: GO BACK TO THE BASICS

Once you have mastered proper technique, the free throw becomes mostly a mental challenge. But it is possible that sometimes you feel something different in your form or throughout your body that makes you feel uncomfortable, affecting both your mechanics and your mindset. Maybe you have not been seeing much playing time, or have not shot the ball from the field well, and now your confidence is not as high as it usually is; maybe you have a little nagging injury or are coming back from time off and feel a little discomfort; or maybe you are both mentally and physically fatigued from the duration of the season. A variety of situations can sometimes lead to a slight shooting slump even at the free throw line. Not where you are missing every shot (your problem would be more mechanical in that case), but where you are simply missing more free throws than usual and are not feeling a sense of rhythm and confidence. This is quite common even at the professional level and it is only human, so don't get alarmed. But you calmly have to address the situation in order to regain your natural confidence and habitual shooting percentages.

To me, the solution is a lot simpler than what you may think. Go back to the basics and give yourself a quick review course of your basic shooting mechanics. Not just one day, but consistently for a certain period until you have regained your natural comfort level and confidence. In any case, slump or not, great free throw shooters incorporate a brief mechanics routine in their every day warm-up or training session just to make sure they are keeping their skills sharp.

You should perform the most basic and elementary technique drills that you practiced when you began learning how to shoot. Initially, you may want to even take the basket out of

Figure 4.8 *Basic technique drills help you regain your rhythm and confidence during a slump.*

BALL-HANDLING

During a so-called shooting slump or period where you are feeling hesitant shooting the ball, in addition to going back to your basic mechanics drills, I have found it productive to incorporate some simple ball-handling drills to reacquire your comfort level and feel for the ball. Consequently your feel for the basket will also improve.

the picture (always visualize yourself making the shot) to remove the pressure of converting the shot. Then once your shooting motion begins feeling smooth and natural again, you should progress to actually shooting at the rim. Always begin in close in front of the basket and move yourself back one step at a time. This is not just a mechanics review to refresh your technique, but also a simple method to see the ball go in consistently as you progress, thus helping you regain your positive mindset and confidence in your shooting ability. Practice one-hand shooting to make sure your shooting hand is holding the ball correctly and giving the right direction; then two hand form shooting, finding your rhythm and stroke, slowly working your way farther away from the hoop back to the actual free throw line.

If your free throw routine has always worked for you, don't abandon it! Stick with it, but slow it down a bit and focus better on each of the steps: this does not mean analyze each step better (as it will cause you to over-think), but don't skip or rush any of them with a superficial approach, and don't become impatient. Patience and proper practice are key to regaining your confidence and form. You cannot afford to be in a hurry.

WATCH WHO YOU LISTEN TO

KEEP AN OPEN MIND AND BE COACHABLE

Being open to too many suggestions can get tricky. You don't want other people to influence you in a negative way, but you also cannot allow yourself to use this as an excuse for not wanting to listen. I have heard several professional and even youth players say "I am not going to change my shot", as if they were hitting shots like Ray Allen. If you cannot make free throws on a consistent basis or are not showing signs of improvement, there is a reason, so don't live in denial. Try to overcome your weaknesses and correct your flaws. You can pretend to be ultra-confident all you want, but it's not going to work if the ball is not going in! Being confident does not mean that you ignore anything "negative" you hear, especially if it is constructive criticism when you are not a great shooter.

Players are often content just being average. For years I thought 80 percent at the free throw line was a major accomplishment, but didn't realize it was just very average and that just a few tweaks could help immensely. What if with just a few minor adjustments you could achieve 90 percent? You must keep an open mind and be open to suggestions, especially if it is your coach who is trying to motivate you to try to reach your full potential. Not being open to constructive criticism and advice that could help you improve is a sign of both stubbornness and uncoachability. Being willing to listen is part of a positive mindset... but at the same time, be careful who you are listening to!

TOO MANY INSTRUCTIONS FROM TOO MANY PEOPLE!

Be open minded and coachable, but remember that you cannot listen to everybody: too

PERSONAL EXPERIENCE

Since I have been in the NBA, I have either seen first-hand or heard of players' struggles at the free throw line. I once trained an NBA journeyman that was well known for his inability to make free throws. Being a solid rebounder, defender and dirty work player, coaches played him for his strengths without worrying too much about his shooting skills. Changing teams every year, or maybe even twice a year, he ended up getting new advice and instructions from countless coaches throughout his career. Too much information and different suggestions just led him to ulterior frustration and no improvement, which is unfortunate because the player wanted to get better.

many opinions and too many suggestions may lead to an overload of information that will cause you to "over-think" everything that you are doing. The more confusion in the advice you receive, the more doubts you will have in your shooting technique and overall development process. I know of many struggling players who got so frustrated with the various directions they were receiving that they had to start tuning people out as everyone, from coaches to personal trainers, from fans to teammates, were offering advice.

As a player you should try working with one coach only. This doesn't mean the one who tells you exclusively what you want to hear, but the one who gives you the best and clearest instruction, yet makes you feel good about what you are doing.

EFFICIENCY OVER ESTHETICS

People will offer their opinions without you asking and perhaps criticize you because you may be doing something "different". But "different" doesn't necessarily mean "wrong". Don't let others' opinions influence your thought process especially if you are capable of making shots on a consistent basis. Be concerned with what matters: efficient shooting mechanics over esthetics. Be worried about a correct technique that delivers a straight shot, not what other people think looks pretty. As we said while introducing shooting mechanics in Chapter 2, great shooters may have different shooting styles but do use the same mechanics for the most part. If you are shooting with proper mechanics and are making shots, and someone doesn't like something in your form, that should be the least of your concerns.

EFFICIENCY OVER ESTHETICS

The two greatest free throw shooters of all time, Guinness World Record holders Ted St. Martin and Dr. Tom Amberry, both showed what you would look at as unorthodox shooting techniques. But they must have been doing something right! Ted made 5221 consecutive free throws in 1996 to break Tom's 1993 streak of 2750 (which was ended on a made shot, but they had to close the gym). I doubt they would care what other people thought about their shooting forms!

Chapter 5

FINDING YOUR COMFORT ZONE: FREE THROW ROUTINE

Finding Your Comfort Zone: Free Throw Routine

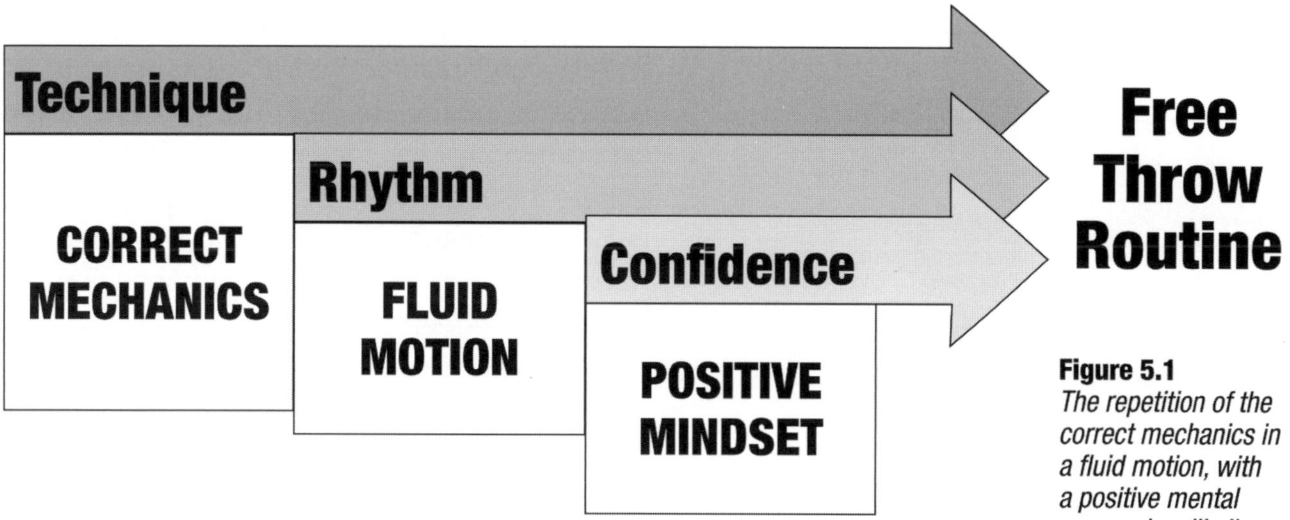

Figure 5.1
The repetition of the correct mechanics in a fluid motion, with a positive mental approach, will allow you to develop an efficient free throw routine.

While I am the biggest believer in using a consistent routine at the free throw line, make no mistake here: your routine does not make shots for you, correct and fluid mechanics and a positive mindset do. Nonetheless, adopting a ritual will allow you to step into your comfort zone, making it easier for you to relax and focus on the necessary steps to making the shot. In the previous chapters we analyzed the mechanical side that is held together by rhythm, and discussed the mental and emotional makeup of the free throw. The positive collaboration of smooth mechanics, body rhythm, confidence, concentration and mental visualization, is in no place more evident than in this setting under the form of a free throw routine. Some of the benefits from developing an efficient routine are:

- The routine eases the mental challenge of the free throw.
- The routine gives you something to focus on rather than thinking of the pressure of making the shot.
- It's the routine's steps that guide you through each free throw attempt.
- The routine actions increase your sense of rhythm before you actually begin raising the ball.
- The routine triggers those automatic subconscious muscle movements that you have rehearsed thousands of times.
- The routine eliminates the over-thinking, uncertainty, doubts, which all lead to hesitation… the last thing you want to occur as you are about to shoot the ball.

CONSTANT REPETITION LEADS TO DEVELOPING A ROUTINE

You have practiced efficiently and mastered smooth shot mechanics, which are now ingrained into your muscle memory. Constant repetition of the correct mechanical movements has led to a fluid and automatic shot motion, which has become second nature. No over-thinking, no hesitation, no tension, no effort, just swishes! Your concentration and confidence have grown and you feel good about your progress and shooting form, and you now walk up to the line with positive energy running throughout your body.

Figure 5.2 *A free throw routine helps you find your comfort zone.*

Good practice habits and repetition at the free throw line lead you to understanding certain patterns and realizing what works for you. At sometime during the learning process, while experimenting and determining what allows you to systematically step into your comfort zone each time you walk up to the line, you have developed some consistent habits that are beginning to feel "right". Shot after shot, make after make, these steps begin to define your shooting routine.

A free throw routine is not a "good luck ritual". Its purpose is to allow you to focus on the right things and step into that relaxing comfort zone, where you believe you are going to make each shot every time you are at the line.

I don't think predetermining what steps to go by is the right way. You just don't wake up one day and tell yourself "my routine is going to be seven dribbles, spin the ball, point to the sky, and shoot… and then fist-bump my teammates". I believe that you fall into the routine process thanks to constant repetition and patterns of success.

A ROUTINE IS PERSONAL: KEEP IT SIMPLE!

All great free throw shooters have their own routine at the foul line. You don't need to imitate anyone else's shot preparation. Although it is always good to observe what successful shooters rely on, free throw rituals are so personal, that it doesn't make much sense to copy someone else's personal habit, since you don't know the process behind it. Most of all, you should stay

Figure 5.3 *Keep your routine simple, consistent, efficient, and automatic.*

away from the flashy exaggerated nonsense that has no effect on the shot or actually complicates things further. The only thing you should try to copy is the simplicity!

I strongly discourage players from playing around with the ball, doing any ridiculous spinning, massaging or excessive dribbling. Ask yourself "what does this do to help my shot"? None of these habits are fundamental mechanical points in shooting, so you should

UNUSUAL RITUALS IN THE NBA

Many famous NBA players over the years have used some unusual or even bizarre routines at the free throw line. Some were good shooters, others were just fair. Just to name a few: Karl Malone, Gilbert Arenas, Jason Kidd, Jeff Hornacek, Rip Hamilton, Jerry Stackhouse, Alonzo Mourning, Adrian Dantley and even Kevin Durant with his famous "shoulder shimmy". Remember that a good shooter makes free throws thanks to his shooting mechanics and mindset, not because of a silly or eccentric action in his routine.

never give in to any absurd rituals other than the basic steps. These actions do not help and sometimes may be what is hurting you. By spinning the ball before you shoot you are giving up one of the most valuable advantages you are given in free throw shooting: the opportunity to position your hands and fingers exactly how you want them for a smoother release. While "massaging" the ball may help you to get a feel for it, it is not necessary, and you are just procrastinating the entire shot release. Same thing for taking 10 or more dribbles: 1, 2 or 3 dribbles are plenty. Just get at it! Don't give yourself a chance to think about more stuff. Go straight to the task at hand!

For a successful free throw routine, you should eliminate the useless time and effort consuming actions. Your shot preparation should be all substance: simple, consistent, efficient, automatic, and to the point. These factors determine a successful free throw routine, not how much you spin, rub, or dribble the ball. Find what works for you. Whether it's one dribble or three, one deep breath or two, a mechanical reminder (like "legs", "straight", "elbow in", "up" or "over the rim"), or a "reassurance" word or phrase you say to yourself, develop *your* routine. I can't tell you what will work for you, all I can advise is not getting too fancy, flashy, or overly creative. The routine must help you feel as comfortable and confident as possible when you step to the line.

FOCUS ON WHAT MATTERS: THE STEPS OF YOUR ROUTINE

The routine will make you focus on each of its steps rather than the outcome or pressure of the shot and the score of the game. In addition, it takes your eyes off the target for a moment, alleviating much of the pressure in your mind. You should never stare at the rim too long to try to focus better. That doesn't work and may actually make you more nervous. Trying too hard and thinking of converting the shot can hurt you, leading you to "choking". Focus on the routine's steps to relax while picturing a perfect shot, with the ball right above the goal about to swish through the net, in your mind. Focus on the journey not the goal, let the routine accompany you: process over product.

10 SECONDS TO PREPARE AND DELIVER YOUR SHOT

For each free throw you have 10 seconds to prepare your feet and hands, focus, aim, and release the basketball. This is plenty of time, so you don't need to rush your shot motion, but you shouldn't wait too long either. In no way do you need all 10 seconds to prepare for the shot. No free throw routine should take more than 6 or 7 seconds for its execution. As soon as the referee hands you the ball, you should step into your routine. The more you wait to shoot the ball, the more over-thinking and hesitation may come into play. Eliminate all the fancy show nonsense: get your feet positioned, take a few dribbles, grip the ball, locate the rim and shoot. Don't waste time messing around with the ball, massaging and spinning it around; there is no use for more than 2-3 dribbles. Most of all, don't stare at the rim throughout the 10 seconds you have at your disposal as it can add unneeded pressure in your mind. Locate the rim, but don't focus on it too long. You know where it is and what it looks like, as you should have a clear mental picture of the goal (with the ball about to swish through it) in your mind at all times. Once you locate the rim and begin the extension sequence, keep your eyes focused on the basket until the ball has gone through it. There are some great shooters who do follow the flight of the ball, usually on long distance shots, but in any case, I would never recommend that (*see Follow-Through/Vision in Chapter 2 – The Mechanical Side*).

LET THE SHOOTER FOCUS !!!

I've always endorsed the finger pointing after a nice pass for a basket, the high fiving after a nice play, hugs after a substitution and all that. But what's the story with all the fist bumping and touching hands after each foul shot nowadays? Am I getting too old school here? It was bad enough when teammates would go up to the shooter after each shot, but now it's actually the shooter who reaches out both arms and hands to get a little love from the two rebounders, whether he made or missed the shot! Why do we want to add something extra to think about? While I am a huge supporter of anything that enhances teamwork and camaraderie, this is absurd. What does it do? Reassure the shooter? Let him concentrate for God's sake! You can fist bump, hug, kiss, dance, and party after the game. During the game, let's focus on making free throws and winning the game!

Figure 5.4 *Focus on the steps of your routine, not the outcome of the shot.*

CONSISTENCY IS KEY

The common denominator to all good free throw routines is consistency. The ritual should always be exactly the same and not rushed. The more we do something, the more natural and automatic it becomes. Your preparation, thought process and shot motion should be so effortless and automatic that you are relying more on muscle memory than actually thinking about the shot. Focus on the steps of the routine, not the outcome of the shot. Let the routine guide you through each free throw. Automatic motion every time!

Don't change your routine every time you miss a shot. You can't over-analyze every shot. You must recognize why you missed, but immediately erase it, and picture the next shot being on target. If you are missing left and right, it's not because the routine is faulty, it's because your mechanics are faulty. Anything long or short is easy to correct with a slight adjustment for an accurate make on the next attempt.

RECOMMENDED GUIDELINES AND CHECKPOINTS FOR YOUR ROUTINE

Simple, consistent, efficient, automatic, and to the point – that's what you are looking for! While you must develop your own personal free throw routine, you should follow certain guidelines. These are the main checkpoints that have worked for me, and which I recommend:

- **STAY OFF THE LINE** - Until the rest of the players set up and the referee is ready to hand you the ball. Waiting for everyone to take their places can lead to anxiety or impatience, and cause you to think.
- **STEP INTO YOUR ROUTINE** - As soon as the referee hands you the ball.
- **ESTABLISH YOUR SHOT LINE** - Locate the nail (or the middle of the rim) as it is a good reference point. Set your feet so the strong side of your body is aligned. Take a quick look at the rim to make sure you are centered.
- **FIND YOUR BALANCE** - As soon as you get your feet placed, you should slightly bend your knees, but without exaggerating your flexion at this point. Although many players take their dribbles before they bend their legs, I prefer you to be already somewhat "loaded". Do not focus on the rim yet.
- **DRIBBLES** - I do not recommend more than three dribbles as anything more is totally unnecessary and useless. Your last dribble should lead you into your stance: flex your knees, hips and ankles a little more so you get under the ball with your hands in position to shoot.
- **GRIP THE BALL** - Once you pick up your last dribble, you should grip the ball so that your shooting fork (index and middle fingers) is in the middle of the ball. Place your hand so that your shooting fork is in the seam and straddling the ball's inflation valve. Now you have a firmer grip and know your shooting fingers are in the middle of the ball and aligned with the middle of the goal. Wrist should be cocked and the ball is in your shooting pocket (the strong side of your stomach-chest area below the shoulder). Avoid any hesitation from this point on.

PERSONAL EXPERIENCE

Over the years I have continued to reduce the number of dribbles during my free throw routine: from 3 to just 1, and now I use none. This is simply to maximize time, so I can shoot a larger number of shots during my practice session. However, I do recommend you utilize 1, 2 or 3 dribbles, in order to relax and not fall into a trap called impatience!

The next 3 actions should occur almost simultaneously, not necessarily in order: as soon as you grip the ball, you should locate the rim, take one deep breath, repeat your reassurance words, and be ready to raise the ball.

- **LOCATE THE RIM** - You should never focus on the rim throughout the preparation as it just adds unwanted pressure. Once your hands are placed properly on the ball, now is the time to finally turn your eyes to the basket. I recommend locating the rim once (briefly) at the beginning of the routine, to double-check your alignment as you position your feet, and then again when you are ready to raise the ball. "Lock in" from here on, never taking your eyes off the rim. Any time you look at the goal you should visualize the ball right above the rim about to drop straight down the center with a perfect swish. This is a strong mental reassurance component.
- **ONE DEEP BREATH** - At some point during the routine you will need to insert a deep re-

> **BREATHING PATTERNS**
>
> Poor breathing patterns at the line may lead to tightening up, hesitating and releasing a tense shot. Breathing properly can relieve you from any anxiety or nervousness, and allow you to relax. Breathing should be part of your habitual free throw routine.

laxing breath. As you grip the ball and your eyes now turn to the rim, this is the time to take that breath. Inhale, preferably through your nose (although I inhale through my mouth, they say it is more efficient to do so through your nose) and as soon as you exhale (preferably through your mouth), begin raising the ball, while visualizing that perfect mental image of a successful shot.

- **REASSURANCE WORDS** - This is very subjective and you may or may not incorporate a special word to your routine. These words should either characterize the idea of a successful shot or represent a mechanical reminder, such as "straight", "swish", "up", "rhythm", "through", "freeze", etc.

The next 4 actions are to finish the shooting motion

- **RAISE THE BALL** - From your shooting pocket region, raise the ball as smoothly as possible up to your release point – or as I prefer saying at the free throw line, "through your release point" as it emphasizes more of a one-piece motion that extends into your follow-through. Everything goes up together in a fluid, rhythmic extension, with no real pause at your release point.
- **FOLLOW-THROUGH** - Once the ball has reached your release point, your entire body should open up in a fluid sequence. Use an upward and forward arm extension and snap your wrist, thrusting the ball with a confident follow-through.
- **FOOT EXTENSION IN SYNCH WITH ARM EXTENSION** - To maximize positive energy and rhythm, extend your feet without letting your heels drop back to the floor.
- **FREEZE YOUR FOLLOW-THROUGH** - As we discussed in shooting mechanics, holding your follow-through is a good habit and indicates confidence and positive energy going through your shot motion. End with your arms up, fingers inside the rim, shoulders level, balancing yourself on the balls of your feet… and enjoy watching the basketball swish through the rim!

You should realize right away just by "feel" if the ball was released properly, so if you have to, you will make a little adjustment on the following shot.

> **MY ROUTINE STEPS & CHECKPOINTS**
>
> 1. SHOOTING FOOT to the right of the nail (my alignment is inside my foot)
> 2. SLIGHT KNEE FLEXION to feel balance, stability and a sense of rhythm
> 3. GRIP THE BALL with fork in the middle for alignment and wrist loaded
> 4. DEEP BREATH and EYES ON THE RIM at the same time
> 5. RAISE THE BALL THROUGH RELEASE POINT with one smooth motion
> 6. FOLLOW-THROUGH with shooting fork into the rim
>
> CHECKPOINT: Foot Extension / Elbow ends right above eye level
>
> Throughout the routine I maintain the mental picture of a perfect shot.

Chapter 6

COACHING AT THE FREE THROW LINE: TEACHING METHODS AND GUIDELINES

Coaching at the Free Throw Line: Teaching Methods and Guidelines

"In most sports improvement depends on a combination of four factors: physiology, technology, equipment, and coaching. In free throw shooting the first three have either remained the same or are irrelevant. So "coaching" is the one element we need to look at."

– **Ray Stefani**, Sports Statistical Analysis Expert
(speaking on the topic of free throw shooting percentages not improving in over 50 years)

This section is not intended to be limited to just coaches or aspiring shooting coaches, but also players of all levels looking to understand the dynamics behind teaching and learning a good free throw technique. In fact, proper planning and practice leads to the player's ultimate goal of not only making shots consistently, but also learning how to coach himself: understanding reasons for missed shots, making instant adjustments, staying focused, and practicing properly.

Great shooters learn to coach themselves!

Having had the opportunity to observe countless practices and workouts at all levels around the world, I have seen many world class basketball coaches and skills trainers with great qualities: prepared, organized, passionate, energetic, and caring. However, one thing continues to stand out to me: very few know how to address the skill of shooting, and most overlook the importance of shooting mechanics. Very little time is dedicated to free throws during team and individual practice sessions. While at some levels available gym time and practice time may be limited, I still feel that coaches need to take responsibility and hold their staffs and players more accountable: stressing the importance of free throw shooting (remember the five benefits from the introduction?), finding appropriate individual time, addressing each player's individual technique, designing individual programs for improvement, tracking progress, etc. Remember: if you want to see results, free throw shooting should be an important part of both your team and individual practice.

DEVELOP A METHODOLOGY THAT REFLECTS YOUR PHILOSOPHY

1. Establish Your Method's Areas of Importance and Teaching Techniques

2. **Individual Player Shooting Analysis for a Personalized Plan for Improvement**
3. **Follow Certain Teaching Guidelines**

In order to develop your own methodology you will need to figure out what your philosophy consists of, what's important to you in shooting instruction and development, and what your teaching methods are going to be. When it comes to shooting mechanics and the free throw, I can tell you MY areas of importance, priorities, checkpoints, teaching guidelines, reminders and pointers... but this methodology makes sense to me, based on my research and personal experiences. It will be up to you to determine what YOUR philosophy and main areas of concern are. Your teaching techniques represent your philosophy, and define your methodology. You cannot predetermine what your teaching method is going to be without a defined philosophy and without experimenting.

QUESTION AND EXPERIMENT ALL CONCEPTS, TEACHING METHODS AND DRILLS

Adopting the traditional/preconceived shooting concepts, methods and drills can limit your personal research, experimentation and analysis, and not allow you to see the big picture. You must keep an open mind and flexible approach when teaching shooting, and in coaching in general. Inflexibility limits your creativity, as sticking to the script doesn't allow you to open up and develop your creative side. I expect all readers to question this book's concepts, and perhaps to not always agree, but I do encourage you to experiment, first on yourself then with your players. The more doubts and questions you have, the more you will look for answers and finally determine what the best teaching methods are for you.

ESTABLISH YOUR METHOD'S AREAS OF IMPORTANCE AND TEACHING TECHNIQUES

TEACH TO SHOOT THE BALL STRAIGHT: NO RIGHT OR LEFT MISSES FOR A CONSISTENT SHOT LINE

My primary concern is the player's shot line: helping the player learn how to shoot the ball straight, thus eliminating left and right misses. Since you can basically miss shots four ways (left, right, short, long), by eliminating the misses to the side, you are automatically reducing the chances of error by 50 percent. My philosophy is that a player's confidence will grow almost instantly just by knowing his chances of missing have been cut in half.

A straight shot is a good shot!

I am rarely concerned with short or long misses. When I begin working with a new player, one of the first things I tell him when we hit the floor is "I don't know how to teach you to make shots, but I can teach you how to shoot the ball straight". Don't take this as a given, because for a player, learning how to deliver a straight shot is fundamental for his development. Since the player's shot line is key, we must focus on the mechanical components that allow consistent alignment with the rim throughout the shot motion:

1. **Foot Stance** – We talked about this being personal, but the feet should be facing the rim the best way the player can. Proper balance means stability, which helps consistency for a straight shot. While the general indication is to align the shooting foot with nail and middle of the rim, you should determine each individual player's alignment based on his body structure. For one play-

er it may be the nail, for another maybe 2-3 inches to the side of the nail. Every player is different. Align the ball at the release point (not shooting foot) with the middle of rim, and then adjust the feet accordingly.

2. **Shooting Pocket** – Player must hold the ball with wrist cocked on the strong side of the body as he gets himself "under the ball". No excess movement and/or body-crossing, in order to maximize force transfer straight toward the goal. Ninety-degree angles for a compact technique.
3. **Shooting Hand/Grip** – Comfortable finger spread with shooting fork in the middle of the ball, already pointing in the direction of the rim. No palm on the ball, wrist cocked back.

"Coaching lasts only for a game, but teaching lasts a lifetime."

– Hall of Fame Coach **Pete Newell**

4. **Balance Hand** – Always on the side of the ball, no palm pressure, must not interfere with shooting hand release.
5. **Follow-Through** – Being the last force and direction given to the shot, the player must maintain proper alignment throughout the extension process. Freeze the follow-through with shooting fingers "inside" the rim.

Shooting the ball straight, eliminating the mechanical flaws that cause a right or left missed shot, and reducing chances for errors represent a fundamental concept in teaching a correct shooting technique. It's the main area of focus when coaching both young and professional players at the free throw line. Once a player learns to deliver a straight shot, then it becomes easier to address all other parts that make it possible to convert shots on a regular basis. But remember: as a coach you can design a plan, give directions, reassure and correct, but at some point the player has to figure out some things on his own. You can give the player all the ingredients, but ultimately he will need to put everything together. Once you have gotten them to no longer miss shots to the right and left, they will need to understand how to put the ball in the basket. A lot of personal aspects like rhythm, confidence, concentration, feel, depth perception, arc, and angles come into play now. It takes time and practice to master the free throw shot, but in no way is it possible without having learned how to shoot the ball straight first.

WHERE DO YOU START? WHAT ARE YOUR PRIORITY AREAS?

As you establish your main areas of importance, you must also determine which parts of shooting mechanics you should prioritize, especially since you may only have a short period to work with a player. In my opinion, the beginning and ending of the shot motion are the most important and first to address: player's foundation and follow-through positions. Be concerned with how players establish their base, position their feet and hold the ball in their shooting pocket. Then check how they extend and finish the shot, how and if they use their feet as they release the ball. The in-between mechanical defects (let's say a flying elbow at release point like Reggie Miller) are usually less conditioning than the extremities' flaws: as we saw in our

LEVEL OF THE PLAYER

The coach's priorities and main areas of attention may differ according to the level of the player. While with beginners you may address more the basics of the feet, balance, one hand shot release, and alignment, with advanced shooters you might focus more on the little details to polish their mechanics and to stimulate their minds.

mechanics section, an efficient follow-through may fix a previous mechanical flaw that occurs during the shot motion.

We want to start from the ground and work ourselves up. I feel it is best to begin with what can be adjusted or corrected in the player's foundation position, without touching the shot motion itself. This way the player feels less threatened as you are not addressing his actual shooting form, which is a very sensitive area. Example:

- **Foot Stance** - Are the player's feet turned or pointing at the goal? Does he lead with his shooting foot? Does he establish the same foot position on each shot?
- **Balance** - Is the player in a good balanced position? Are his feet shoulder-width apart? Is his weight distributed equally on both feet? Is his head above his base of support? Does he get under the ball? Is his core activated?
- **Basic Alignment** - Does the player look to establish the same alignment every time or is it just proximal? Stand behind the player to make sure all the components are aligned with the rim. Have him load the ball to his forehead/eye area as a test (like a shot fake) to check what kind of alignment he has at his release point.
- **Hand Placement and Grip on the Ball** - Does the shooting hand have a comfortable finger spread, fork (index and middle fingers) in the middle of the ball with wrist already cocked back? Firm but not tense grip on the ball for proper control. Balance hand on the side of the ball. Neither hand puts any palm on the ball.
- **Excess Movement** - Make sure the leg flexion is not exaggerated. Elbows close to sides, compact position, under the ball, not exposing it. No unwanted ball movement in the shot pocket area. Eliminate the unnecessary nonsense in the routine (too many dribbles or spinning of the ball); simplify the technique.
- **Mindset/Approach/Body language** - How does the player carry himself when he steps to the line? Does he look confident or is he hesitant? Would you feel comfortable with him at the line to seal a team victory? If a player does not show the "attitude" it will be hard for him to deliver a successful shot.

Figure 6.1 *Hand placement for a comfortable grip on the ball is a priority area.*

YOUR APPROACH

Acknowledging what the player is already doing well, before you start addressing the mechanical flaws, helps the player feel comfortable with you and your teaching approach. Beginning with the negative issues, the trust factor will be hard to build and may turn the player away.

COMPONENTS	QUICK REMINDERS AND POINTS OF EMPHASIS
BALANCE	Key for consistency because it provides a sense of stability. As important as balance is, it doesn't make shots for the player.
HAND POSITIONING	Comfortable grip with fork centered in the middle of the ball. Wrist loaded, no palm in contact with the ball. Balance hand on side of ball, no interference on the release.
ALIGNMENT	Some players may have to experiment to find a comfortable alignment. A slight turn in stance is fine if it feels right, but limit any "hard" turns or twists. Alignment must be maintained throughout the shot motion.
FOLLOW-THROUGH	Extension should occur with an "up & forward" motion. Stress holding the follow-through, maintaining alignment. A good finish may fix a poor shot or overall shooting technique.
RHYTHM	Rhythm keeps the components together, allowing a smooth shot motion that requires less effort. Hard to teach as it develops within. Player must feel it.

MY PERSONAL REINFORCEMENT POINTS
• **Wrist and Feet** – I am big on efficient wrist snap and foot extension, as these are the two most underrated sources of strength we have, and at the free throw line you do not need to add any exaggerated power from your legs and arms into the shot. I am not much of a "flex your knees more" person: at the free throw line, strong legs are important more for a sense of stability, but not as much for power as they are in jump shooting.
• **Elbow Extension for Proper Arc** – To maintain a consistent arc on the release, I recommend that on the follow-through, the player finishes the motion extending his shooting elbow above his eye level (*see Follow-Through in Chapter 2*).
• **Positive Motion** – I want the player to focus on a smooth "up and forward" shot motion where he imagines his body following the trajectory of the ball into the goal. So I want to see the player's chest slightly forward, balancing himself on the balls of his feet, as he finishes the shot.
MAIN CHECKPOINTS WHILE OBSERVING THE SHOOTER
• Check what the player is doing well: what can you "keep" and build on, and what has to go.
• Check the player's foundation for proper balance, correct angles, activated core, ball position, and a compact stance.
• Check the player's hand and finger position on the ball: look for a confident grip and shooting fork in the middle of the ball.
• Check if the player maintains proper alignment throughout the routine.
• Check the player's head position: does he jerk it back? Do his eyes follow the flight of the ball? Can he see the basket?
• Check the player's follow-through: does he look confident? Full extension? Proper direction, arc, backspin?
• Check the player's foot extension: is the player getting enough force out of the feet?

INDIVIDUAL PLAYER SHOOTING ANALYSIS FOR A PERSONALIZED PLAN FOR IMPROVEMENT

SCOUTING

Any program for improvement begins with knowledge first, so the research in determining "the reasons why" a player makes or misses free throws plays a major role in shooting instruction. Therefore, before designing a personalized plan, a coach must:

- **Observe**
- **Evaluate**
- **Identify**
- **Analyze**

In professional basketball, this type of process is the same as we see in scouting players, the profession I have been in for the past 19 seasons. In recent years I began applying scouting guidelines specifically to analyze the art of shooting: combining my two areas of expertise, player evaluation and shooting technique, to address players' shooting deficiencies. This approach has definitely helped me in both areas of my work, as I believe that good scouting represents the foundation of shooting instruction. A detailed scouting report is the blueprint to an efficient player development plan. If you cannot identify the shooter's habits, preferences, and technical flaws, it will be impossible to determine what to perfect or correct once you get on the court.

FOUNDATION POSITION

Observing a player's foundation position gives coaches a chance to determine if there are any physical or muscular imbalances to address. Often it is a physical component that affects a player's stance, which may complicate his shooting motion.

it, while on film you have the opportunity to freeze the images, rewind, play in slow motion. So by combining both, you can really get in-depth with your research and analysis.

Figure 6.2 *Observation is necessary in order to evaluate a player and design a plan for improvement.*

Both in-person and video (game film or practice footage) can be very effective forms of observation and evaluation. If you are on the court with the player you can get a close look at the player's shot technique as he performs

You must pay attention not only to the fundamental basketball skill components, but also the biomechanical aspects as sometimes it is a physical/postural deficiency that is affecting the player's shooting form and percentages.

The individual player analysis reports I prepare cover all aspects of a player's shooting technique: not only their basic mechanical shot technique, but also free throw routine, game situation preferences and habits, footwork, areas to improve, recommended drills that address needs, etc. Recently I have begun integrating the pure technical basketball side with the modern statistical side (not "nerdy" quantitative data, which does not help players make more shots... but facts that allow a coach to understand why and how players miss shots) supported by video/image analysis. Since the player's shot line is my main area of concern, I believe in tracking and analyzing how a player makes (back rim with ball returning, swish, "dirty", etc.) and misses his shots (long/short, left/right, or combination) to determine certain patterns of success and error. This type of feedback and data allows you to narrow down the mechanical reasons for misses and address the issues in practice.

Figure 6.3 *Tracking shots is a good way to measure improvement.*

Again, these concepts are based simply on my own personal experiences and they make sense to me. I recommend that you determine what is important to you, and embrace your own observation and evaluation analyses in order to identify the areas that need attention. You may come up with different ways to assess the players' shooting abilities, but what's important is that once you take them to the basketball court, you have a clear idea of how to improve their shooting techniques and percentages.

THE POWER OF VISUAL: IMAGES AND VIDEO

It is inherent to my scouting job that I observe players both in person and on video. Whether it's just the daily NBA highlights or actually assessing a player, I do like to spend

"Coaches can talk and talk and talk about something, but if you get it on tape (video) and show it to them, it is so much more effective."

– Hall of Fame Player **Larry Bird**

time freezing images or re-watching a play to understand what a player does right or why he missed a shot. Seeing yourself shoot for the first time can be as shocking as hearing your voice on voicemail. "Is that really me?!" you may say. Video is a powerful tool in today's world, and you can use it as a major teaching tool in shooting instruction. While I do not use them all the time, both video and images can be very efficient methods to address a player's technical issues without turning him away. Since shooting, especially free throws, is such a sensitive topic with players at any level, you need to watch how you approach the player. This method puts the player in charge for a moment as you are basically asking him "what do you see?", so you don't appear to be too critical, insistent or aggressive. By "reversing roles", the player feels in a position of control, and becomes more open to suggestions, recognizing his flaws and realizing what he needs to address in order to improve. Now you guys are working together to design a plan for improvement, and the player knows you are there to help him.

To film a player, there is no need for any sophisticated equipment or software. I usually use a video application called "Coach's Eye" on my phone or tablet, which I can instantly use on the court or show the player after the session.

SPEAK AND TEACH THROUGH IMAGES

I keep a number of images on my tablet that represent and promote key shooting components, or show common mechanical flaws. Whenever I see a significant photograph that I feel I can use to reinforce what I preach I save it. At some point during the coaching journey, we must reduce verbal instructions, and using images is a terrific method to deliver teaching points, without "harassing" the player. This helps him realize what he may be doing incorrectly and also reassures him of what he is already doing welll.

Figure 6.4
Using video and images is an efficient teaching method.

During the observation process when you are still scouting your shooter, make sure you film him from all angles: front, back, and both sides. If necessary, you can also do close ups (all angles) of the lower body or upper body motions to really be able to see any particular details.

PERSONALIZATION

Once you have observed and evaluated your shooter, it will be easier to understand how to proceed in your teaching. Every player is different and you will need to design a personalized program that fits each one's needs. All shooting forms evolve differently depending on individual coordination and body structure in terms of height, size, strength, arm and leg length, hand size, shoulder width, etc. As a coach you cannot expect every player to comfortably adopt the same exact shooting principles you teach or use yourself, even if they are correct. Understanding a player's biomechanics, body parts and limitations (tall, uncoordinated, weak, past injuries) is extremely important in order to tailor a technique to each shooter's needs, based on their physical structure and abilities. Here are a few common modifications made to suit the needs of particular individuals:

- **Limited Strength** - Especially with younger players, don't be afraid of lowering a player's shot pocket and setting the release point to the clavicle/shoulder area, below the eyes instead of above. *See "Players with Limited Strength" in Chapter 2 for more options.*
- **Big Hands** - Less spread between fingers so that the player doesn't cover so much of the ball. Make sure this new hand grip doesn't permit any palm contact on the ball.
- **Long Arms** - Set the player's release point higher, above the head instead of right above the eye. Make sure the shooter doesn't bring the ball behind his head, and that he keeps proper alignment.
- **Long Legs** - Shaky legs will cause knees to cave inward. Reduce (never eliminate or you may lose sense of rhythm) knee flexion to avoid instability in the legs which can compromise balance.
- **Wide Shoulders** - Players are probably not as flexible in their upper body. Have them widen their shooting elbow a bit because they probably will not be able to keep it under the ball. Perhaps even a slight stance rotation will be necessary in order to find a better alignment with the basket.
- **Past Injuries** - A previous thumb, wrist, shoulder, or elbow injury might affect a player's grip on the ball and/or shooting form. Evaluate which modifications you can adapt to the player's technique.

THE BASIC FUNDAMENTAL MECHANICS

While you may not be able to teach each player the same exact shooting form, as many will develop their own "personal" styles, you must instill consistent guidelines that stress the same basic fundamental mechanics.

SAMPLES OF SHOOTING ANALYSIS REPORTS

Establishing a non-dominant side shot pocket can cause several issues:

- *Fingers are misplaced on the ball, and not within his basic shot line.*
- *Right elbow pops out from his hip and it is no longer aligned with the rim.*
- *Wrist is not properly loaded.*
- *Excess motion (crossover motion) as he must raise the ball across his body (vision also compromised).*

We want to reduce possibilities of mistake, searching for an efficient economy of motion. Shifting his initial ball position from right, to left, back to right, just adds more movement and chance of error somewhere during the shot. He needs to focus on his dominant side for a simpler motion that remains consistent and within his shot line.

Despite a good arm extension on his follow-through, he is dropping back on his heels immediately, thus pulling his shoulders and head away from the basket. In order to eliminate this "negative movement", and develop a more positive "up & forward" shot motion, he needs to focus on extending his feet as he follows-through, and remaining in balance on his toes with his chest slightly forward as he finishes the shot.

FOLLOW CERTAIN TEACHING GUIDELINES

Here are a few fundamental teaching guidelines that you should always keep in mind and try to follow while coaching at the free throw line.

EMPHASIZE THE IMPORTANCE OF FREE THROW SHOOTING

Make a big deal about free throws! Players need to know, coaches cannot forget. Hold your staff and players accountable. Stress the five reasons to practice free throws from our introduction: 1) improves mechanics; 2) develops confidence; 3) more team wins; 4) more playing time at end of games; 5) more points to the box score even on a bad night. These should remind the players of the importance of the shot, but also motivate them to work at it. A player's shooting technique needs daily attention, practice and repetition to stay sharp. Free throw shooting must be a key ingredient to both team and individual practice. Too often I see players mentally unplug at the end of practice and free throw shooting becomes a social event. Don't allow your team and yourself to accept a superficial approach and settle for mediocre results as if they were actually of high standard.

As a coach you need to stay on top of it. Whether you are working with one player or an entire team, be organized and try charting/tracking the players numbers. Try to develop a sense of pride in your team, and create some competitiveness during practice and workouts. By creating a competitive atmosphere, you also develop teamwork: have players compete as singles, pairs or groups… or just one player with himself (goal driven challenges). Players bond when they are pushing each other to win something even as small as a free throw contest. One day it's one player carrying a group, the next day it may be another. Mix the groups up, make it fun, challenging and competitive. Join in the drills or games at times. Keep track of shots and post weekly rankings (on the locker room wall for example): official game shooting percentages and practice results; I guarantee that players will begin getting super competitive and it will drive your team. Always look for ways of motivating the players: give out awards and prizes at the end of the season to your best performers and most improved.

SHOOTING INSTRUCTION IS DONE ONE-ON-ONE

Of all the game's fundamentals, shooting is the one that is most sensitive to players at any level. Free throw instruction and mechanics practice in general should take place in a calm, private and intimate setting, as I believe that efficient teaching and learning is done one-on-one: one coach and one player. Addressing correct shooting mechanics for a good free throw technique and routine, I strongly recommend teaching just one player at a time. Group shooting is more for shooting repetitions or competitive drills when there is no actual instruction involved. It's hard to address each player's technique flaws in group practice as no player has the same exact needs as another. Each player deserves the proper attention in order to maximize practice time and see the results of their hard work. In addition, a one-on-one environment allows you to connect with the player, developing a sense of trust and teamwork.

Free throw instruction is a different setting and atmosphere than your typical shooting workout. The mental approach and focus are not the same as with game speed shots. With basic shooting mechanics and free throw training there is no high energy as it occurs away from the game's regular up and down the court tempo. Although there is less physical demand, the level of attention and focus is at its highest. Not high energy, but high concentration. You pick it up as you transition into game moves and shots. In fact, as you move forward into more of a repetition and gamelike phase, adding players and creating a group environment is appropriate. Involving another 1 or 2 players in shooting repetitions creates an atmosphere of both competition and teamwork (player vs player challenge and/or team goals)

You Pass, You Rebound - In free throw shooting, the coach should rebound and pass to the shooter as this helps to strengthen the bond with the athlete. However, at times a helper can be useful so that you can observe the shooter from different angles: sides, behind. Sometimes you see things better from a new angle or further distance. With close range shooting drills and free throws, I always recommend that coaches pass the ball to the player using a bounce pass as this allows him to "get under the ball" with his shooting wrist already cocked back.

One Voice - You know where each player is coming from, and what he needs to be working on in order to improve his shooting technique and raise his free throw percentage. You don't want too many people around offering opinions and suggestions. You lose a player when he hears too many opinions. If you are the one teaching, it's your voice only. Not another coach's, not a teammate's, not a buddy's. The player has to get used to and trust your instructions, your voice.

Connecting with the Player / Bonding through Teamwork - A one-on-one setting allows for you and the player to connect and bond. There are many ways to catch the player's atten-

Figure 6.6
During form shooting and free throws a bounce pass is recommended.

tion in order for him to really listen to you. What is your strength? It may be your presence or personality, your playing career or resume, your ability to knock down shots or demonstrate, your knowledge and communication skills. Whatever it is that makes the player buy into your coaching, you need to sell the "we process": stress "we" over "you" or "I"! Coach and player working together, in it together. Players must sense that you have been in their shoes and that you care. You connect with a player once he knows you are "in" 100 percent and you believe in him. Always use the first person plural, for example: WE are trying to accomplish; WE are getting there; WE gotta stay focused; WE are seeing great improvements; WE are missing short, etc. You have to match the player's effort physically, mentally and emotionally.

Shooting with the Player - One way that has helped me connect and bond with the players I have worked with has been shooting with them. Over the years I have realized that as a coach you have to maintain ways of keeping the players' attention and both motivating and stimulating them. And for me there is no better way than joining a player, youngster or professional, in free throw practice, usually at the end of a workout or occasionally by jumping in during a session. You don't want a too loose or friendly atmosphere, but sometimes you need to spice things up or make it more competitive or even entertaining. While challenging a player has its pros and cons (you never want to humiliate your own student… unless he gets too cocky!), I love to team up with a player in order to try to reach a "team goal". For example: hitting 18-20 fouls shots, two shots at a time for each one of us. This helps in several ways:

- The player has a consistent model (demonstrator) in front of him.
- Bonding: you can strengthen the relationship with your players, as they feel you are in it with them.
- Builds teamwork: pushing one another, helping one another.
- Builds competitiveness: even with a team goal, it's good for players to want to shoot the higher percentage and not be the one who misses the last shot to reach that goal.
- Builds leadership: with time, the player will learn to "carry" the group (coach and player, or other players).

Figure 6.7 *Joining a drill can help you connect and bond with the player, and stimulate competitiveness and teamwork.*

BONDING THROUGH TEAMWORK IN SHOOTING DRILLS

I have a fond memory of the relationship a player and I built a few years ago. A professional player, Alessandro, was struggling with his foul shooting and we began working on it. After a few weeks of coach-player free throw shooting at the end of our sessions, things started getting pretty challenging and competitive. I set the goal of making 19 out of 20 free throws to end practice. Alternating shooting two free throws at a time, we reached 20 for 20 and then decided to continue until there was a miss. 40 for 40, 60 for 60.... we finally reached a combined 100 out of 100 (50 for 50 each) and I decided to end the session on an extremely positive note as it was a great team accomplishment. I enjoy the memory of that session, and consider it a great example of relationship bonding. I also view it as the highest level of teamwork, and also competitiveness: neither one of us wanting to miss, neither one wanting to let the other one down, and despite fatigue after a two hour workout, we both wanted to see how far we could go. 50 consecutive free throws may not be much of an individual achievement, but 100 as a team is an outstanding accomplishment.

REASSURE AND REINFORCE THROUGH POSITIVE COACHING

Even the greatest shooter may run into a little frustration from time to time, and need some sort of mental or emotional reassurance. Players can be extremely sensitive in the learning stages of training, while correcting and/or automizing proper technique and mastering the free throw shot: it is very common for players of any level to get discouraged, frustrated, and doubt both themselves and the process. This is where both the coach and the player are challenged on a personal level, and you must watch how you handle your student. Although in teaching free throw technique the energy is not high, you still need to motivate, reassure, reinforce and energize the player. Tell him to keep his head up, never show signs of lack of confidence: never shake his head, never let his chin drop to his chest, never start cussing. Good shooters learn to keep their composure, controlling their emotions. They recognize the mistake, make the instant adjustment and forget about it, and always believe they will make the next shot. Self control and discipline are paramount, so don't allow your player to "lose it".

As a coach, although you may be focused on fixing the negative issues, it's a good idea to praise what the shooter is already doing well and how you are going to build on from that. Tell him that you have seen other successful shooters that had the same issues, but were able to overcome them with proper adjustments and that he can do the same. You cannot only address the negative or what is keeping him from being a good free throw

"The master coach is highly skilled at making the players feel good about themselves."

– Hall of Fame Coach **George Raveling**

HIT 'EM UP WITH A TEXT

The reassurance and reinforcement doesn't end with your practice session. If a player had a great session and his confidence is high, send him a text message: "great job today", "keep up the good work". If you feel a player's frustration, write him something encouraging: "don't get discouraged, it's a step by step process", "you are laying the foundation, results are coming soon", "you can be a great shooter".

shooter. The player needs to know that you believe in him, if not he will not believe in himself. The free throw can be an emotional shot, so use positive rather than negative words that will encourage and reassure your player. Reinforce the positive and remind him of the improvements he has already made and how he is headed in the right direction. Once a player feels good about what he does well, it is easier to "trick" him into fixing the mechanical flaws in his shot mechanics.

Making the Adjustments - Try not to make an observation or adjustment every time a player makes a mistake. Sometimes it's better to do so after a number of times he commits the same mistake. This way you are giving your shooter a chance to realize what and where the error is on his own... then you acknowledge his adjustment, praising him. Always allow your shooter the opportunity to correct himself when possible without your intervention.

During the observation and planning process you have to understand where there are actual mechanical flaws and where there may just be an esthetic flaw: before you make a mechanical suggestion or correction, make sure that there is an actual issue. Common examples: an off hand turn (it may turn as the ball is already out of his hands), a flying elbow (he may bring it in on his release), or a non-shooting arm drop (he may drop it when the ball is already in mid-air). Sometimes an apparent flaw does not affect the shot despite not being esthetically pretty to watch. The last thing you want to do is take a player out of his comfort zone and add doubts to something he is doing successfully.

Use Positive Terminology - With free throws being a sensitive area, I have learned to avoid any sort of terminology that can turn the player away from you. Negative or intimidating words are not always well received, especially at an advanced level. Substitute words like "change" and "correct" with more positive terms like "improve" or "better". Limit the "don'ts" and "nos", and refrain from any sarcastic comments or negative body language as the player will feel it and eventually tune you out. Be an optimistic and positive presence and speak in terms of: improvement, achievement, adjustment, perfecting, mastering, polishing, etc.

Practice Time - Commitment to practice is key, and the player has to embrace it. The first improvements and results a player sees are in the practice setting. It may take him longer for these improvements to transfer to official games, so always reassure him and reinforce the "journey" concept, and that success is around the corner. The player must leave practice thinking that he is a great shooter in the making and that he is improving. Always end your session on a positive note, reaching even the simplest goal, so there is a sense of accomplishment and the player's confidence will carry over to the next day.

SIMPLICITY IS YOUR GUIDE

"Keep it simple. When you get too complex you forget the obvious."

– Hall of Fame Coach **Al McGuire**

With teaching free throws, I believe the coach's job is to help simplify the player's shot technique and routine. Focus on what matters, eliminate the unnecessary. Less is more: less movement, less thoughts, less nonsense… more baskets! Precise instruction with simplicity as your guide: simple phrases, simple terms, simple concepts, simple mechanics, and a simple free throw routine. You lose the player with too much information and a fancy vocabulary. Your player is not as experienced as you are, so don't get too complex and elaborate, if not he will think that a free throw shot is harder than what it actually is. So use simple terminology that players can relate to and assimilate more easily.

YOUR VOICE

Verbal instruction is the main method of communication in teaching basketball. Your voice is a tool, but you have to be careful how you use it: excessive talking can be counterproductive, as players may eventually tune you out, no matter how great your message is. You can sometimes replace verbal instruction with demonstration, which can be more effective in that it is visual. As we saw earlier, another alternate method is to "speak through images" that represent key teaching points in shooting technique (both correct and incorrect aspects).

WHEN DEMONSTRATION TAKES OVER

The ability to perform and demonstrate a basketball skill and/or drill correctly is one of the most powerful teaching tools and methods in sports. Not only does it attract the player's attention and give the coach instant credibility, but it is also an efficient method of communication and instruction, that can take over for the often redundant verbal communication.

KNOW THE "WHY" BEHIND YOUR DEMONSTRATION

Let's make no mistake here: whether you were a good player or not, being able to demonstrate is an enormous coaching skill. But you have to understand the dynamics of the fundamental skill behind your correct demonstration and execution, if not your teaching becomes sketchy or incomplete. Knowledge and preparation are paramount in your demonstration.

The mediocre teacher tells. The good teacher explains. The superior teacher demonstrates. The great teacher inspires."

– William Arthur Ward

Figure 6.8 *Being a great demonstrator can take your teaching to another level.*

In shooting instruction specifically, having a consistent model in front of the players to observe and study can be very useful and help the teaching, motivating and learning journey tremendously.

INTRODUCING A NEW TECHNIQUE

Making adjustments in a player's free throw technique is not always easy, especially with an advanced or adult player. You have to warn him that there will be a struggle between his brain and his muscle memory patterns. Although the brain understands the new instructions and what to do, the muscles may continue to do what they have done for years. Because of this inner struggle, there is a strong chance

Figure 6.9 *Be detail oriented while introducing a new technique.*

The Process of Teaching and Learning a New Skill:

1. Coach explains what he is looking for
2. Coach demonstrates the correct execution
3. Coach observes the player's execution
4. Coach corrects and/or perfects the player's execution
5. Player repeats the correct execution over and over

for a brief regression phase, while re-training your muscles to develop a new muscle memory. This is why it is so hard to change a player's shot the older and more advanced he becomes. It takes time, patience, so there must be a plan.

ATTACK A "BAD TECHNIQUE" THAT IS NOT WORKING

There is a common belief that you cannot address mechanical flaws in a player's shooting technique during the basketball season because it may have a counterproductive effect hurting his confidence. While in some cases I would tend to agree, if a player has one or more major flaws that are preventing him from making shots, why wait? He can't get much worse, and you need to attack the problem. Start from the bottom, work yourself up: if you can fix anything in the beginning and ending of the motion, you have already done something. If a player is a decent shooter, but could be better and you do not want to mess with his mind and an average free throw percentage, so be it... but if a guy can't make shots now, you may as well face the issue sooner rather than later.

TAKING THE RIM OUT OF THE PICTURE

Don't be afraid of taking a struggling player out of the group. Sometimes in order to progress in a positive manner it's best to have him shoot away from the basket in order to correct his mechanics: shooting to himself, shooting at the wall, etc. Taking the rim and the pressure of making the shot out of the picture can help a player not lose his confidence. Repeating an incorrect shooting form, and consistently missing, is damaging to the player's mindset. In addition, you don't want him to feel inferior or embarrassed in front of the more advanced shooters on the team.

Shooting to yourself away from the basket allows a player to focus exclusively on the mechanical parts and the rhythm of the shot motion, without the pressure of converting the shot. This way, the player avoids feeling discouraged and doubtful with his new technique until he has mastered it and it has become automatic.

Although there is not a rim involved, you should stimulate the player to use his imagination to visualize a perfect shot with the ball swishing through the net. The entire process should reinforce positive thinking and mental imagery, keeping the player's mindset sharp.

"LET ME SEE YOUR FORM" (without the ball)

When a player has a "choppy" shot technique, ask him to show you his shooting form, without the rim and without the ball. Just imagining loading the ball and releasing it. In most cases the player will perform a more correct and smoother, more fluid shot motion. Ask him if this feels more natural. You can use this as a building block, trying to recreate this same shooting form step by step with the ball in his hands, searching for the same fluidity the player showed without the ball.

PATIENCE

I should be the last person to preach patience! I am the guiltiest person in the world when it comes to being impatient, both on and off the basketball court. I often have to remind myself of the process and that there is no instant satisfaction in shooting development; it takes time to see results. Learning is a step by step process and you and the player must expect possible setbacks. You cannot get discouraged at the first hurdle. Stay patient.

In my first book, *Shoot like the Pros,* we introduced the concept of a progression training model to follow, or to at least keep in mind during practice. In *Mastering the Art of Free Throw Shooting* we presented a development model that featured a "perseverance phase", to remind you that you must persevere with your training as it takes time to see measurable results.

WHAT DO YOU DO WITH A HIGH PERCENTAGE FREE THROW SHOOTER?

My first reaction to the question would be "leave him or her alone". But, my idea of high percentage may be different from what the player thinks. If we are talking about an 85-90 percent game foul shooter, he probably doesn't need any suggestions or need to change what he is doing. But I believe a coach can always challenge or stimulate a player further, giving him higher practice goals. If someone shoots 90 percent, he is doing something right and it's probably not a question of proper mechanics…. But why not motivate him to reach 95 percent!? Focus on the little details, and push him to beat any preconceived mental limitations he may have, like believing it is impossible to do any better.

WHAT DO YOU DO WITH AN UNORTHODOX FORM BUT HIGH PERCENTAGE?

I am often more intrigued with those successful shooters that use an unorthodox technique, than the purest shooters of the game. If someone's free throw form breaks most of the basic fundamental rules, and still manages to convert at a high level, he must be doing something extremely right! I wouldn't say anything, especially if I haven't yet figured out exactly how he is making the shots. But I have found it very rare that a player with an unusual but successful shot technique does not rely on at least two of the basic four fundamental components (*see Chapter 2: balance, hand placement, alignment, follow-through*). Perhaps add that he has great focus and confidence, and you got yourself a great free throw shooter despite a funky form. I have yet to see a player using unorthodox form, with shaky balance, poor hand placement, broken alignment, and weak follow-through make any type of shot. So, when a player shoots the ball oddly, check his main shooting fundamentals and you may find that he is actually using some of the key components of a correct form. Jamaal Wilkes, Shawn Marion, Bob McAdoo, Reggie Miller, Kevin Martin are primary examples. Derek Fisher was a player who had a lot of wasted motion in his technique, and I would never teach that type of shooting form. But if you analyze his foundation position, it is correct; he grips the ball well; he has a consistent shot line; if you check his follow-through, he has a tremendous extension and release (*remember: beginning and ending are your priorities*). So despite an unusual form with lots of excess motion (having long arms and wide shoulders), he was still a good shooter.

In the next chapter we will go over some basic mechanical drills along with other exercises and competitive games that will help enhance your players' shooting form and free throw percentages. Remember: all drills are important and key to improvement, but it's the details of your teaching within the drills that make the difference.

50 COACHING TIPS AND REMINDERS

1. Make a big deal about free throws and stress their importance. Hold your staff and players accountable!
2. Great coaches are outstanding teachers. Be a teacher first!
3. Stay in shape! Your credibility and professional image are important.
4. Be a great demonstrator, take pride in your craft.
5. Use terminology the players can relate to.
6. Use simple and precise instructions.
7. Use positive language, avoid the intimidating terms that may turn off the player, or hint that you don't believe in him or her.
8. Keep a positive body language: player has to know you believe in him; if not, he will never believe in himself.
9. Establish a comfort level first: offering criticism and/or suggestions can backfire if you have not yet developed a relationship of trust.
10. Let the player find his comfort zone. If there is a drill a player is good at and it makes him feel comfortable, let him go to it in order to keep him confident.
11. Add a positive reinforcement when you can.
12. Keep practice setting intimate, limit distractions!
13. Distinguish instructional one-on-one practice, from multiple player workouts and team practice. There is a big setting difference between shooting instruction (teaching) and shooting reps.
14. During both team practice and player workouts, make sure that free throw shooting is under gamelike conditions: no socializing, joking around, allowing setting to become too loose. In order to make it gamelike, you can't interrupt the player. Wait until he has shot and he is rebounding for a teammate, or take him out of the group for a quick tip.
15. Ball-handling has a key role in shooting development. Good grip comes from a good feel for the ball: include basic ball-handling drills in your daily warmup routine.
16. Don't underestimate the physical component in shooting.
17. You have to question philosophies and concepts that you may have inherited and always thought were true.
18. Don't adopt a new teaching point, method, or drill without questioning it and experimenting with it.

19. Experiment on yourself. Always look for answers.
20. Always know the WHY behind your teaching methods and instructions.
21. The observation/evaluation process is the foundation of your instruction. Observe your player from the feet up. Analyze the reasons why a player misses shots, so you know what to work on.
22. Don't try to over-analyze each shot, don't try to correct each shot. Wait until the player repeats the same mistake several times, so you give him a chance to figure it out on his own first. If he is capable of making the necessary adjustment by himself, praise him!
23. A straight shot is a good shot.
24. Mechanics drills are important and most of them are good, but it's the details in the instruction that matter most.
25. Use a bounce pass while rebounding and passing the ball to your shooter during mechanics and free throw training. This allows the player to not shoot in a hurry and to get in the habit of getting under the ball and cocking the wrist on the catch.
26. Use model players who are similar in size, athleticism and position as your student.
27. Every player is unique and different physically, mentally, emotionally and represents a new project. Personalize a program for each and every player.
28. Be organized, keep notes.
29. Follow your method's progressions.
30. Track shots, keep totals in order to monitor progress and quantify improvements.
31. Save images you find online, in magazines, etc. that show key fundamental mechanics and teaching points you stress.
32. Video and images: not only do they help you analyze mechanics, but are powerful tools to reach the player.
33. Examine all angles of the player's technique: front, back, both sides.
34. For your team's growth and to increase competitiveness within the group, create a big board that tracks practice and game free throw numbers. Nobody wants to look bad, and it stimulates players to get better. At the end of the season, give prizes not only to the best, but to who shows improvements.
35. Be honest, speak the truth. At the same time, however, be encouraging.
36. When a player thinks he knows it all and is resistant: let him fail. You cannot help someone who doesn't want help. Remain available, but don't force yourself on him.

37. Be flexible: don't insist when things are not going as you had envisioned them. Sometimes you need to move on or simply end the session.
38. Allow the natural adjustments the player makes if they prove to work. Don't correct an unorthodox but naturally instictive technique.
39. Join the drill or competition at times: the player may need a challenge or is fatigued and needs a teammate to help, push or carry him.
40. Make it fun for the younger kids. Their level of concentration is not as high as adult players. Reward their effort with a little fun.
41. Learn on the job: hold camps and clinics, offer private lessons to young kids, experiment.
42. Set goals to avoid boredom, to motivate and to create competiteveness.
43. Don't sell unrealistic results and improvements even if they are just for motivation. Set progressive goals in order to see measurable step by step results.
44. Give high level shooters high level goals.
45. Water breaks: have the player shoot two (or even 1 or 3 at times) free throws before water, and next time maybe right after water.... or even no water, just a quick break. This helps simulate a gamelike time out, technical foul or a brief interruption.
46. End practice on a positive note, reaching goals, and finishing with two consecutive perfect shots.
47. Know when to end the session: missed shots and frustration due to mental fatigue can hurt the player's confidence.
48. You cannot make shots for your players. Give them direction, accompany them, but at some point they need to figure things out on their own.
49. Always stress the "journey" concept to a struggling player. Step by step process.
50. Some players just don't have it... Do the best you can to help them improve, even if just slightly.

Chapter 7

PRACTICING AT THE FREE THROW LINE: TECHNIQUE DRILLS, EXERCISES AND GAMES

Practicing at the Free Throw Line: Technique Drills, Exercises and Games

"Excellence is the gradual result of always striving to do better."

– Hall of Fame Coach **Pat Riley**

You cannot expect to see results in games until you have mastered the shot in a practice setting first. Before you can become an elite free throw shooter in games, you need to become one in practice. While I have seen players shoot well in practice and not be able to do so in games, I have never seen or heard of a player who was great in games and not very good in practice. Your journey to success starts with practice: mastering correct shot mechanics, and practicing on a daily basis, challenging yourself to reach the highest level imaginable.

In order to become an elite free throw shooter you have to practice as much and as regularly as possible. Develop great work habits using consistency as your guide. Practice with a purpose, not just to get through the drills, as you can never be in a hurry. Focus on the details to polish your technique. Each free throw shot must be gamelike, so you need to recreate the game's setting in your mind. Always end your session on a positive note, or at least on two clean consecutive made free throws. Watch who you surround yourself with: do not workout with inconsistent people or poor workers as they will be dead weight for you.

As we saw in Chapter 4, the Mental Side, mental practice through visualization/mental imagery and also watching short video clips of yourself converting shots, can be of additional help throughout your journey.

YOU CAN'T FIND THE TIME?

It takes just 12 minutes to shoot 100 free throws and one hour to shoot 500 shots, and that is if you are rebounding for yourself. If you and a friend partner up and rebound for one another, you can get up 250 free throws each in much less than one hour… so no more excuses! Get to work!

DEVELOPING YOUR DAILY WARMUP ROUTINE

Every time I am on a basketball court, I see both younger kids and older players, walk on the floor and immediately start jacking up long distance shots as soon as they grab a ball… needless to say with poor results. All successful shooters have developed a basic daily warmup routine they go through in order to keep their skills sharp and their mind focused, whether it is a 5 minute habit or a more thorough 30 minute version. Very rarely do I see a veteran Pro player even attempt a jumper or long distance shot before going through a little warmup practice, brief or simple as it may be. This may include a few ball-handling drills or push-ups to get hands ready, or just a simple series of form shooting drills to refresh proper mechanics. Always begin close to the basket to find your comfort zone and progressively move back.

You can't be in a hurry to dive into game shots or even free throws. Once you begin feeling comfortable and confident, then you are ready to transition to jump shooting and free throw practice. By preparing properly, progressing one step at a time to find your groove, once you get to the free throw line, the goal will appear much larger and it will seem as easy as shooting a lay-up.

You can vary, condense, expand your daily warmup routine depending on available time and how you feel. What's important is that you find consistency in what you do and develop good habits. If you have not shot for an extended period, you may want to devote a little more time to your basic drills. Develop your own daily warmup routine and stick with it.

GETTING YOUR OWN REBOUND

While it does become boring and time consuming, rebounding for yourself during free throw practice also has advantages for your improvement.

1. **Foot Position:** retrieving your own rebound gives you the opportunity to reset your routine (first step is always setting feet correctly) and re-adjust your feet every time.
2. **Patience:** with a rebounder/passer you may fall into an impatient and hurried motion as you will tend to speed up your routine. Going to get your own rebound, the timing and step by step routine process is easier to follow and more gamelike.
3. **Positive "Up and Forward" Shot Motion:** all positive forces for a fluid shot are enhanced. Knowing that you need to go get your own rebound you will subconsciously lean and fall slightly forward, as if you were following the trajectory of the ball into the goal (not to be confused with "following your shot"). With time you will learn to control and balance your body, finishing up on your toes.

TAKING THE RIM OUT OF THE PICTURE: SHOOTING TO YOURSELF AWAY FROM THE BASKET

Shooting the ball to yourself away from the basket is a basic drill which allows you to focus exclusively on the correct mechanics without the pressure of converting the shot. This way, you avoid feeling discouraged and doubtful of your new shooting technique until you have mastered it and it becomes automatic. You may perform this exercise in front of a mirror, shooting to the wall or simply up in the air. What's important is that you imagine yourself executing a game free throw, focusing on your mechanics and the steps of your routine. Although there is not a rim involved, you should always use your imagination to visualize a perfect shot with the ball swishing through the net.

SHOOTING MECHANICS DRILLS TO MASTER PROPER SHOOTING TECHNIQUE

Being the ultimate mechanical shot, we must focus on basic mechanics drills that help perfect a proper "stand still" shooting technique, which eventually will lead you to improving your overall shooting abilities. In fact, we will re-propose many of the same mechanics drills that were introduced in my ***SHOOT LIKE THE PROS: The Road to a Successful Shooting Technique book***.

Remember: all shooting drills are good and can be productive, but you must focus on the mechanical details involved in order to get the most out of them and see improvement. You can adjust or modify all the drills and games in this chapter as you see fit throughout your journey. Set goals to self-motivate and avoid boredom.

FORM SHOOTING DRILLS

Perform drills starting close to the basket and move out progressively. If you are a beginner or are working to make adjustments to your shooting technique, you might need to begin "away from the basket," shooting the ball straight up in the air to yourself. As you feel more comfortable and confident in your new mechanics, perform using the basket.

ONE-HAND FORM SHOOTING DRILL

This drill improves your ability to control the ball, your feel for it, and proper one-hand release. Practice this in your basic basketball stance, in balance, with legs and hips flexed and the ball in your shooting pocket area. There are two versions:

1. Feel the ball as it lays in your shooting hand and find a good grip. Then raise the ball up to your release point, rotating your hand

Figure 7.1 *One-hand form shooting drill.*

and forearm to the correctly aligned shooting position. Keep your shoulders squared and shoot the ball. Hold your follow-through.

2. Use your balance hand to help prepare the shot while holding the ball in your shot pocket. Find the proper grip, and with your shooting hand only, raise the ball up to your release point. Keep your shoulders squared and shoot the ball. Hold your follow- through.

Your goal in both versions of this drill is to make the ball go straight to the basket as you have no balance-hand interference. Knowing that you have eliminated right and left misses will boost your confidence in your shooting technique.

Progression: Shoot to yourself, away from the basket, and then shoot at the basket. Begin at close range and then move back.

ONE-HAND FORM SHOOTING WITH BALANCE HAND DRILL

Use your balance hand to prepare the shot and raise the ball up to your release point. Take the non-shooting hand off of the side of the ball, keeping that arm up, and release the ball one-handed with a good follow-through.

Progression: Shoot to yourself, away from the basket, and then shoot at the basket. Begin at close range and then move back.

TWO-HAND FORM SHOOTING DRILL

Same as the previous drill, but now with your regular shooting form, using both hands. Release the ball, making sure that you use a clean one-hand release, avoiding any balance- hand interference.

Figure 7.2 *One-hand form shooting with balance hand drill.*

Figure 7.3 *Two-hand form shooting drill.*

Progression: Shoot to yourself, away from the basket, and then shoot at the basket. Begin at close range and then move back.

ON YOUR BACK SHOOTING DRILL

Lie on your back with the ball positioned right above your strong-side armpit, your shooting elbow on your side (it's okay if it touches the floor), and your hands/fingers in correct position with shooting wrist already cocked. Release the ball vertically up in the air, letting it fall straight back into your hands in their original position. Focus on extending your shooting arm straight up with good fol-

Figure 7.4 *On your back shooting drill.*

low-through, wrist snap, and backspin. Almost every aspiring player has tried this while lying in bed fantasizing about making a big shot!

CHAIR SHOOTING DRILL

Sit in a chair with your back straight. Begin close to the basket and move back progressively. Prepare your shot with correct hand placement and proper alignment in your shooting pocket, then shoot the ball—extending your arm with a good follow-through. This drill will make you rely on the strength of your back, shoulders, shooting arm, and wrist, so you will exaggerate your follow-through. As a result, you will also improve your shooting range.

Progression: Shoot to yourself, away from the basket, and then shoot at the basket. Begin at close range and then move back—never to a distance so far that you must alter your technique by straining yourself or throwing the ball, compromising your shot line.

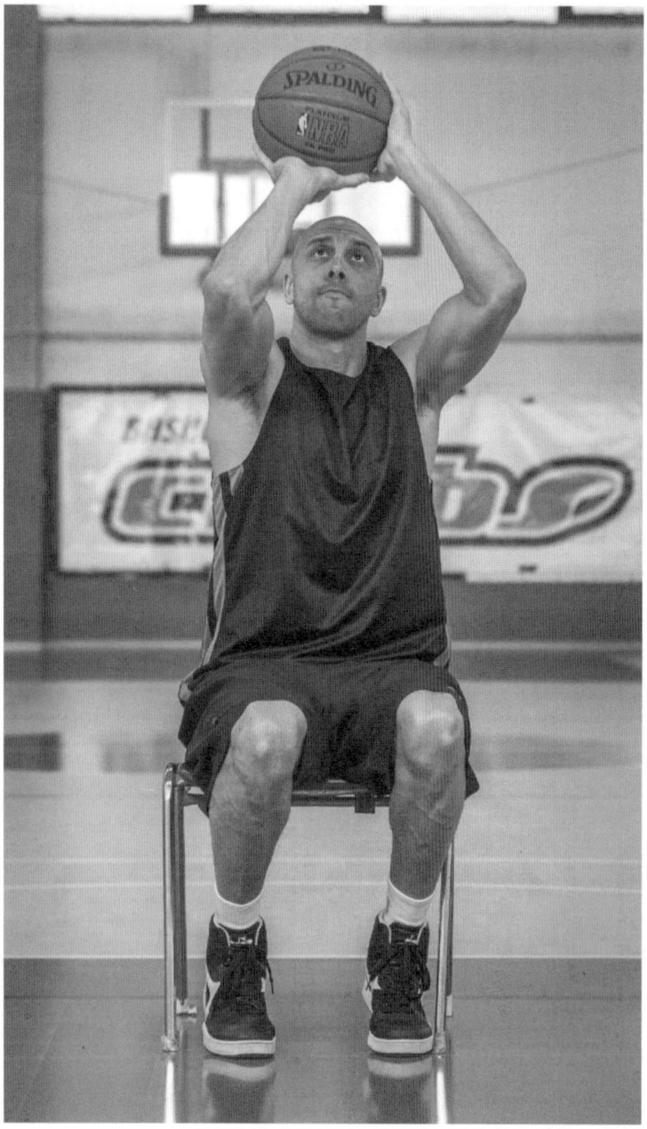

Figure 7.5 *Chair shooting drill.*

FLOOR SHOOTING DRILL

This drill is a progression from the chair shooting drill as now you are further challenged by sitting on the floor with your legs either crossed or open. Only players with the appropriate upper-body strength should utilize this drill. Perform following the same guidelines as in the chair shooting drill.

Progression: Shoot to yourself, away from the basket, and then shoot at the basket. Begin at close range and then move back – never to a distance so far that you must alter your technique by straining yourself or throwing the ball, compromising your shot line.

Figure 7.6 *Floor shooting drill.*

WRIST-ONLY DRILL

Stand in front of the basket with your shooting arm fully extended and the ball laying in your shooting hand with your wrist cocked. Shoot the ball exclusively with the use of your wrist, making sure you get proper force and rotation. Finish your shot by putting the two shooting fingers "into" the basket. Younger kids who are not able to get the ball over the rim can just shoot to themselves away from the basket following this procedure.

Figure 7.7 *Wrist only drill.*

SHOOTING ALIGNMENT DRILLS

ELBOW-IN DRILL

Hold the ball in your shooting pocket (stomach-chest area on strong side) with hands in shooting mode, elbow and forearm always at an approximately 90-degree angle. Focus on the strong side of your body, feel your elbow in, touching your hip. Like in your shooting motion, smoothly raise the ball up above your

Figure 7.8 Elbow-In drill.

eye as if you were pump faking, and then lower it back down again, making sure your elbow just gently brushes your hip (no friction), therefore not "popping out." Repeat.

UNDER THE BALL + ELBOW-IN DRILL (WITH A PARTNER)

One player stands in front of the other, 10′-12′ apart. One passes the ball to the other using a "bounce pass" (best in order to get low). Lower yourself to get under the ball in a correct compact basketball stance as you catch the pass with hands "ready": loaded wrist and shooting fork in the middle of the ball. Focus on the strong side (shooting side) of your body, with all components aligned and feet facing your partner. At this point, raise the ball like in the previous "Elbow-In" Drill: transfer the ball from your shooting pocket to your release point, as if you were pump faking, and return to initial position. You may do this 1 or 2 times, making sure that your elbow remains in (gently brushing your hip) throughout the drill, and that your hands do not change position on the ball. Pass the ball to your partner (or coach) who will do the same.

Note: Good drill to use with large groups or in a basketball camp setting when there are not enough baskets available.

LINE SHOOTING DRILL (WITH A PARTNER)

Find a straight line on the basketball court (half-court or sideline, for example). One player stands 10′-12′ in front of the other with the shooting foot placed on the shooting line or just to the side of it based on his/her typical routine. Shoot the ball back and forth to each other (us-

Figure 7.10 *Line shooting drill.*

Figure 7.9 *Under the ball + Elbow-In drill.*

ing a realistic arc), letting it bounce on the line or as close as possible. Focus on aligning your body parts, ending the motion in balance on your toes, and holding your follow-through to develop a consistent and straight shot line.

Progression: One-hand to two-hand form shooting.

Note: Good drill to use with large groups or in a basketball camp setting when there are not enough baskets available.

SIDE OF THE BACKBOARD DRILL

Stand to the side of the backboard, 10′–12′ away. Align your body and shoot the ball, aiming at a spot at least 10′–12′ high on the side of the backboard. A correct release will make the ball come back to you.

Progression: One-hand to two-hand form shooting. Begin at close range and then move back.

Figure 7.11 *Side of the backboard drill.*

WALL SHOOTING DRILL

Stand 10′–12′ feet in front of a wall. Aim at a spot 10′–12′ high on the wall. Shoot the ball (without throwing it, and using proper arc) at the spot you are aiming for. Focus on proper alignment, follow- through, and finger control. A correct release will make the ball come back to you.

Progression: One-hand to two-hand form shooting. Begin at close range and then move back.

Figure 7.12 *Wall shooting drill.*

SHOT LINE FEEDBACK DRILL

This exercise is useful for advanced shooters who are already making the majority of their shots, but are looking to stabilize their shot line. Using some athletic or colored tape, tape down the middle of the paint. On every converted shot, check where the ball bounces once it comes out of the net. This exercise gives you instant feedback on your alignment.

Progression: One-hand to two-hand form shooting. Begin at close range and then move back.

DRILLS TO DEVELOP SHOOTING RHYTHM

CHAIR SHOOTING DRILL 2

This is a progression of the Chair Shooting Drill on page 126. Sit on a chair, 10′–12′ in front of the basket. Prepare your shot with correct hand placement and proper alignment in your shooting pocket, then smoothly rise to a standing position and release the ball in a fluid manner, ending the shot in balance on your toes while you follow through. This method allows

Figure 7.13 *Shot line feedback drill.*

Figure 7.14 *Chair shooting drill 2.*

you to coordinate your leg motion with your arm motion, thus developing shooting rhythm. As a result, you will also improve your shooting range.

Progression: Begin at close range and then move back.

PROGRESSIVE FORM SHOOTING DRILL

Begin in front of the basket with 1-hand or 2-hand form shooting. Your feet may not leave the floor. As you begin making baskets and feeling good about your shot, move back a step and do the same. After you start making shots from the new position, step back again and again, until you find the limit of your shooting range (the point when your technique breaks down and you begin altering your basic mechanics). This drill will force you to progressively use your feet and lower your release point and overall technique more as you move farther back. Make sure you keep your alignment and basic technique consistent.

Note: It is okay to fall slightly forward initially.

Figure 7.15 *Progressive form shooting drill.*

This drill will constantly challenge the limits of your range, stabilize your shot line, and you will learn how to use your power sources efficiently. You will improve your shot rhythm and general coordination, feel for the basket, and depth perception. In addition, this is a great every day confidence building exercise as making shot after shot as you move back progressively, you begin to see the basket get wider and wider.

Note: This drill should be part of your daily warmup routine.

SPEED SHOOTING EXERCISE

You never want to be in a hurry at the free throw line. However, in the repetition phase, while perfecting and automizing your shot motion, speed shooting can be a productive exercise. While I am not recommending speeding up or rushing your routine, this exercise helps to reduce the thinking process as you are relying on a more instinctive/automatic release. Remember, this is not "hot potato" where you are trying to get rid of the ball as quickly as possible; you want to continue shooting the ball with proper form, just at a quicker pace, shot after shot.

For this exercise a rebounder/passer is required.

Progression: Begin at close range and then move back progressively to the free throw line.

DIP DRILL (FOR PLAYERS WITH LIMITED STRENGTH)

Prepare your hands, arms and body like you do with your regular shot (see Two-Hand Form Shooting Drill), positioning the ball in your shooting pocket. You may prefer a slightly wider foot stance/base in this drill. Keeping the ball close to your body, lower it below your waist and quickly raise it back up and into your shot for a smooth one-piece motion. You must coordinate this dipping action with your leg motion and maintain your alignment. This drill can help you gain extra power and momentum going into the loading sequence and improve your shot rhythm and shooting range.

Figure 7.16 *Dip drill.*

Progression: Shoot to yourself, away from the basket, and then shoot at the basket. Begin at close range and then move back.

CIRCLE DRILL (FOR PLAYERS WITH LIMITED STRENGTH)

Same procedure as the Dip Drill, but you generate even more power and momentum into the shot, by dipping with a circular "out, in and up" motion. Remain as compact as possible. The movements must be coordinated fluidly with your leg motion to gain maximum power, if not it becomes counterproductive.

Progression: Shoot to yourself, away from the basket, and then shoot at the basket. Begin at close range and then move back.

HOP DRILLS

These "hop drills" are designed to develop proper body balance and control, coordination and shooting rhythm, so as to build a fluid shot motion. Although free throw shooting does not involve jumping, I feel these drills can help your development and aid in understanding your body motion better, which is key in any type of shot. Perform these drills from the middle of the paint, 10'-12' in front of the basket, using a two-foot hop in the following patterns and combine with the ball positions described below:

- **Stationary hops** - Three hops in the same spot, shooting on the last one.
- **Forward hops** - Three forward hops, shooting on the last one.
- **Side hops** - Three hops to one side, shooting on the last one.
- **Forward-back-forward** - Hop forward, hop

back, hop forward again, and shoot the ball.

- **Back-forward-back** - Hop backward, hop forward, hop back again, and shoot the ball.
- **Side-return-other side-return** - Hop to one side and back, then to the other side and back, and shoot the ball.

Ball position progression: Begin holding the ball directly at your release point (above shooting eye) and shooting the ball. You will not be able to perform this drill very far from the basket. Progress by lowering the initial ball position further (shoulder, then shot pocket), adding more arm motion, which will require greater arm and leg coordination.

FREE THROW GAMES AND CHALLENGES

You can perform these games by yourself, challenging a partner, or in a small group of players.

SWISH CHALLENGE

This drill forces you to become a total perfectionist at the foul line because you are not only trying to convert the shots, but also wanting them to fall straight down the middle of the basket without hitting either the rim or the backboard. And even though you might not be reaching the drill's goal initially, you will still be improving your overall free throw mechanics, routine, confidence, and percentage. Each swish (only net) is worth +1 point, each miss counts as -1 (thus setting you back), and each made shot that is not a swish (touches the rim/backboard before falling in) is worth zero points. As you improve you may change the values and make it even more challenging.

Beginners: goal is to reach +5 points.

Advanced: goal is to reach +10 points.

Note: It is possible to shoot 100 percent and never reach the goal of the drill!

PLUS/MINUS GAMES (BEAT THE PRO)

This game forces you to compete against yourself (or an imaginary professional opponent – let's say Kevin Durant). Each time you score a free throw you get one point, but each time you miss a basket you lose two points. Play games up to +10 or +20 points, depending on your level.

Beginner Level: +1 point each made shot,
-2 points each missed shot.

Intermediate Level: +1 point each made shot,
-3 points each missed shot.

Advanced Level: +1 point each made shot,
-5 points each missed shot.

Pro Level: +1 point each made shot,
-8 points each missed shot.

"25" GAME

Your goal is to convert a certain number of free throws (25) with only a predetermined number of possible missed shots, example: you are allowed 5 misses to reach 25 made shots (you must make at least 25 out of 30). You can adjust this drill based on your level, thus raising or lowering the number of made shots and/or possible misses: 25-5, 25-4, 25-3, 25-2, 25-1, 25-0. Over time, this exercise helps you gain confidence in seeing that you are reaching the goal with fewer shot attempts.

CHALLENGING A PARTNER

Competing with a partner can raise the level of the workout and can help you avoid boredom. Some days you might have to push a friend; other days your friend will be the one to carry you if you're fatigued. You can work on a "mutual goal," which helps build teamwork. For example, together you must score at least 18 out of 20 free throws or you can challenge each other in competitive games, shooting 10, 20, 30, or 50 shots (two at a time is best, but you can vary) each. Whoever scores the most baskets out of the number of attempts wins. If you end in a tie, continue until somebody misses; this will increase the level of pressure on each shot.

However you play, focus mainly on sets of two shots at a time each. You should also play occasional games with sets of three shots each (as if you were fouled on a three- point shot), and also one shot each (as if it were a technical foul or an "and one" shot after being fouled on a made basket). Variations are welcome as long as you keep the challenge games realistic and competitive.

GOAL ORIENTED CHALLENGES

Setting goals is self-motivating and also avoids boredom. Goals keep you focused and build a competitive spirit. In addition, reaching goals gives you a sense of satisfaction, knowing you have worked hard. It is better to set progressive objectives, instead of unrealistic ones. You should have goals that reflect the level of shooter you are, and can always raise them as you progress. Avoid high number goals initially, as you may unplug mentally if it takes too much time to reach them. For example, making 10 for 10 free throws 10 times, is more productive than aiming for converting 100 for 100 free throws at once.

CREATIVE CHALLENGES

Get creative and challenge yourself. Mix free throw series with game shots from other areas of the floor, or add a conditioning factor. Anything that challenges your abilities and builds competitiveness with yourself, I feel is a good exercise to train you technically, mentally, emotionally and physically.

Examples:

- Make a certain number of free throws (let's say 10), then hit a Top of the Key 3 point shot, return to the line, and do it again. Try to do this 5 or more times.
- Make one 3p shot from 5 or 7 shooting positions, then go to the free throw line and make 2 out of 2 shots. Try doing this 5 or more times.
- Make 2 out of 2 free throws run to the other baseline and back (1-2 times) to the free throw line for 2 more shots.

Chapter 8

FREE THROW POINTERS, CHECKPOINTS, REMINDERS, MISCONCEPTIONS, TOOLS AND DEVICES

Free Throw Pointers, Checkpoints, Reminders, Misconceptions, Tools and Devices

In this final chapter you will find some additional information in the form of pointers, checkpoints, and reminders at the free throw line, along with common misconceptions about shooting; I have also included a list of useful tools and devices that can help you in your development into a great free throw shooter.

POINTERS ON FREE THROW SHOOTING

- Surround yourself with other hard workers.
- Make free throw practice as gamelike as possible. Use your imagination to recreate game setting and sensations.
- Don't get superficial and be in a hurry to finish your sets. Don't cheat yourself.
- Walk to the line with a confident attitude and body language.
- Don't rush: you have 10 seconds for each shot.
- Don't think about the outcome of the shot.
- Don't stare at the rim throughout the entire routine.
- Let your routine guide you through each free throw: automatic motion every time.
- Don't change your routine every time you miss a free throw.
- Focus on one shot at a time, don't think about the goal to reach.
- Straight misses are usually good shots that require easier adjustments.
- Right and left misses mean your technique needs a mechanical correction.
- Short misses are often signals of lack of confidence, indecision or tension somewhere.
- A good follow-through promotes positive rhythm and is a sign of confidence.
- Long misses, if straight, are not necessarily poor shots, but often have to do with arc, wrist flexion or release point position.
- Don't follow the flight of the ball.
- Your first shot is the most important mentally. You can always make an adjustment on the second attempt. A missed second shot may give your team an offensive rebound opportunity.
- You should never miss two free throws in a row. And most of all, you should never miss two shots in the same manner.
- Vary number of shots during your free throw sets.
- Know when to end practice. Recognize fatigue before you ruin your workout.
- Always leave practice on a positive note regardless of how you shot the ball that particular day. End on two consecutive perfect shots.
- Incorporate mental practice and/or watch brief video clips of yourself shooting the ball to reinforce positive imagery.
- Chart your shots, keep track of your practice sessions.
- "Focus on the journey, not the destination".

QUICK CHECKPOINTS AND REMINDERS AT THE FREE THROW LINE

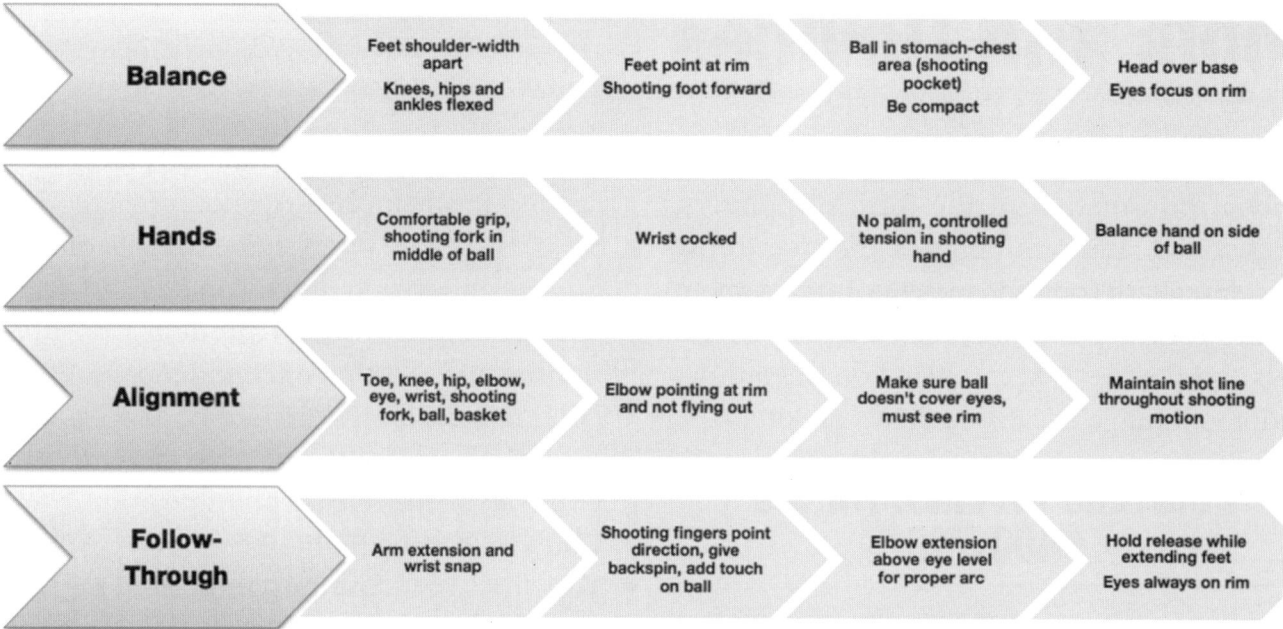

Balance	Feet shoulder-width apart Knees, hips and ankles flexed	Feet point at rim Shooting foot forward	Ball in stomach-chest area (shooting pocket) Be compact	Head over base Eyes focus on rim
Hands	Comfortable grip, shooting fork in middle of ball	Wrist cocked	No palm, controlled tension in shooting hand	Balance hand on side of ball
Alignment	Toe, knee, hip, elbow, eye, wrist, shooting fork, ball, basket	Elbow pointing at rim and not flying out	Make sure ball doesn't cover eyes, must see rim	Maintain shot line throughout shooting motion
Follow-Through	Arm extension and wrist snap	Shooting fingers point direction, give backspin, add touch on ball	Elbow extension above eye level for proper arc	Hold release while extending feet Eyes always on rim

Shooting Rhythm
- Keeps the components together, allowing a smooth shot motion that requires less effort
- Everything goes up together from a proper shoooting pocket position with an "up and forward" motion. No hesitation and/or hitch
- A strong core stabilizes the lower and upper body motions

MISCONCEPTIONS IN FREE THROW SHOOTING

- **"Align your shooting foot with the nail"** – While the nail itself is a good reference point to establish your alignment, most players usually need to position their shooting foot slightly to the right or left of it.
- **"Begin your shot motion from your shoulder area"** – Unless you are at least 6'7", it is very hard to create power and rhythm from a high shot pocket. It is more efficient to begin your shot in your stomach/chest area.
- **"Keep your elbow perfectly under the ball"** – This is an ideal, which is not always possible as it may be uncomfortable for you. Your elbow can be slightly out (not flying out) as long as it doesn't compromise your alignment and you are able to bring it in as you extend during your follow-through.
- **"Your thumbs should form a T on the ball"** – While many coaches teach this rule when addressing the balance hand position on the ball, I feel that it does not apply to most players, especially if they have large hands. Hand positioning on the ball is a very subjective matter, but your priority is establishing a consistent grip with your shooting hand. The balance hand should adapt accordingly, so that it remains on the side of the ball and no part interferes with the shooting hand and the release.

Figure 8.1
Balance, proper hand position, alignment, and follow-through for a fluid shot motion.

- **"Raise the ball above your head"** – A very high release point may cause an unwanted pause and break your rhythm. Worse yet is raising the ball so high that you end up bringing it almost behind your head. Ideally, you should bring the ball up to right above your shooting eye.
- **"Aim at a specific part of the rim"** – While this is a very subjective matter, I believe that the mental picture of the ball right above the rim about to swish through, is a better approach and represents a positive image. Never focus too much on the rim before you begin to raise the ball.
- **"Release the ball off your index finger"** – It is virtually impossible to release the ball solely with your index finger. Position your index and middle fingers (your shooting fork) in the middle of the ball so they can give the last touch and direction.
- **"Bend your knees more"** – There is a difference between using your legs and bending your legs more. Establishing a good stable stance is a big asset in shooting, while exaggerating knee flexion (never more than 45 degrees) may slow down and/or chop your shot motion.
- **"Raise your shooting arc"** – You definitely don't want a flat shot, but an exaggerated arc may cause the ball to approach the rim at a higher impact speed, losing that "touch" that could allow for a soft bounce.
- **"Drop your shoulders back"** – In jump shooting, it can become natural to kick your feet and land slightly forward, and as a result your shoulders may sway back. The free throw is a static shot with no elevation off the floor, and it becomes much more fluid if you focus on an "up and forward" body motion as if you were following the trajectory of the ball into the goal. In no way should we add any negative movement that pulls us away from the basket while shooting a free throw.
- **"Follow your shot"** – While I hear this more regarding jump shots, occasionally I hear someone say it even at the foul line. You never want to anticipate a miss! Focus on your routine and a confident follow-through until the ball reaches the rim.
- **"Big hands are a limitation in shooting"** – This is false in most cases as it is rare to find a player whose hands are so big that he cannot control the ball. Poor feel for the ball and poor shooting technique are limitations, not big hands. Just ask Michael Jordan or Arvydas Sabonis...
- **"You should never address shooting mechanics during the season"** – This is a big cop out excuse you may hear and it drives me nuts. With jump shooting I would be slightly more careful, but for basic free throw mechanics, I always recommend attacking the problem. If you have a faulty shot technique and need to improve or adjust it, chances are you are not shooting a very high percentage in any case, so it's not like your confidence/results will suffer much by addressing the issue immediately.
- **"Use all 10 seconds at your disposal"** – Having 10 seconds to shoot a free throw shot means you are in no rush, not that you need to slow your motion down and attempt to focus or stare at the rim more. Develop an efficient "to-the-point" routine: a few dribbles and get to it. In no way should your preparation take more than 6 or 7 seconds to release the ball.
- **"Practice free throws with your eyes closed"** – While this may be an interesting challenge for good foul shooters, I don't find it to be a productive exercise as you don't shoot blindfolded in real games. Why com-

plicate things? Keep the process and routine as simple and consistent as possible.

- **"The free throw is an easy shot"** – By now you know that this misconception was the premise for me writing this book! It may be easy to become an average foul shooter, but it takes a lot of work and practice to become a great one! Hopefully this book will help you master the art of free throw shooting!

SHOOTING TOOLS AND DEVICES

I have never been a big lover or promoter of most basketball shooting tools and devices. However, here is a list and brief description of the ones that I do like and feel can be helpful in your development into a consistent free throw shooter.

- **"Perfect Jumper"** – This is a device that attaches to the rim, making its diameter smaller. I like the smaller rim concept better than the larger ball, which I am not a fan of (it is not realistic, being a different size than the ball you play with, so it has a different feel, grip, and control than an actual game ball). The Perfect Jumper is a great tool that is ideal for good shooters who need a little challenge. The new rim forces you to become a perfectionist, therefore challenging your aim, shot line, arc and concentration.
- **"Shooting Strap"** – This is a restraining device designed to prevent your balance hand and thumb from twisting and interfering with the shot. It can be a useful tool if players have that tendency.
- **"Free Throw Trainer"** – This is a device that attaches to the front of the rim, helping the shooter to more consistently stabilize the shot line. The Free Throw Trainer gives indications for direction, distance, arc and aids you during the aim and focus process.
- **"QuickShot"** – This is a ball-return device that attaches to the bottom of the rim and funnels the ball on your made shots back to you. This tool allows you to save time and energy rebounding the ball yourself.
- **"Str8 Shooter"** – This device is designed to fit your shooting hand so that your wrist can only move back and forth, eliminating any lateral instability, and stabilizing a straight shot release and follow-through toward the rim.
- **"Weighted Basketball"** – This ball is identical to the standard game basketball, but is heavier (there are 3 lb. and 6 lb. balls). It is not designed for free throw shooting and long distance shooting. However, at close range and for adult players, it can be a helpful tool to reduce movements for a more compact and efficient shot motion. In addition, I find it very useful for ball-handling drills to develop stronger arms, hands and fingers, and also a better feel and grip for the ball, which are all keys for better shooting. While a light medicine ball can also work for some of the same purposes, it does not have the same feel and you must make sure you are using the right weight.
- **"Coach's Eye"** – This is an easy to use tablet application that I use to film and dissect players' shot techniques *(see Chapter 6 – Teaching Methods and Guidelines)*. It is a useful tool for both players and coaches as it allows you to film and break down key images, use slow motion, rewind, freeze images, etc. and also draw, edit, save, and email.
- **"ShotTracker"** – This is a new shooting tool, in the form of wearable tech and phone/tablet application, that automatically tracks every one of your shot attempts, makes and misses. Tracking your results allows you to measure improvement over time.

ABOUT THE AUTHOR

Adam Filippi is the Director of Global Scouting for the Charlotte Hornets, after spending 10 seasons with the Los Angeles Lakers and winning 3 NBA championship rings. Before joining the Lakers in 2001, he was the youngest scout in the NBA with the New Jersey Nets in 1999, then founded and ran Global Vision, an international scouting service that consulted with various NBA teams and European clubs.

As a player development coach, Adam has worked with over 100 NBA and overseas professional players. In addition, he has served as a shooting consultant for various teams, coaches and agents seeking help for their players. Specializing in shooting technique, and a world class free throw shooter himself, ***Mastering the Art of Free Throw Shooting*** is Adam's second book on the skill of shooting. In February 2011, he released his first instructional basketball book ***SHOOT LIKE THE PROS: The Road to a Successful Shooting Technique***, with a foreword by Jerry West, which has been translated into several foreign languages, and is considered by many coaches to be the best book on shooting ever written. A Certified Personal Trainer and Performance Enhancement Specialist by the National Academy of Sports Medicine, Adam has conducted camps, workshops and clinics in the USA, Spain, Italy, China, Ireland, Sweden, United Arab Emirates and more, to teach fundamental basketball skills to players of all ages and levels.

www.adamfilippi.com ■ twitter: @adamfilippi ■ youtube: adam filippi ■ www.facebook.com/adam.filippi.3
■ instagram: adam.filippi ■ www.facebook.com/coachfilippi